Uneclipsed

About Shadows, Emerging, and Finding the Light

melinda hardin

Published in association with Per Capita Publishing, a division of Content Capital®.

ISBN 13: 978-1-954020-20-7 (Paperback)
ISBN 13: 978-1-954020-21-4 (Ebook)

Library of Congress Cataloging-in-Publication Data
Names: Hardin, Melinda, author.
Title: Uneclipsed / Melinda Hardin
Description: First Edition | Texas: Per Capita Publishing (2022)
Identifiers: LCCN 2022903032 (print)

First Edition

Uneclipsed

Total eclipse. August 21, 2017.

For my girls, Celia and Annie.

Table of Contents

Introduction 1

Eclipsed by Approval 11
Body 12
Clean Kitchen 18
Binge 22
Betrayal 25
Home Inspection 29
Paper Cuts 33

Eclipsed by Emotion 39
Embodiment 40
A Letter Regarding Unrealistic Expectations 43
Trend 47
Anxiety 50
Shame 54
Dirty Little Secret 57
Imprints 62

Eclipsed by the Past 67
About Brent 67
Front Stoop 70

Dumpster 73

Him 76

Ben 78

Hot Mess in the Hotel Lobby 81

Eclipsed by the Present 85

Trinity of Tense 86

Mix Tapes 88

Question Quota 92

Any Given Day 95

Standing Guard 99

Loretto 100

Eclipsed by the Future 105

Her Song 105

Medley of Memories 108

Guru 110

Mama Sage 114

Eclipsed by a Shadow 119

Lifesaver 120

Silent Songbird 122

Alli 125

Perspective 128

All of Us 132

Limelight 135

Eclipsed by Addiction 141

How It Happened 142

The Hardest Thing 147

Jesus and Larry 148

Ever Again 150

No Finish Line 152

Two Years Sober 154

A Toast to the Ordinary 155

Eclipsed by Routine 159

Tidal Locking 159

Crescendo 163

Car Fix 168

Circle 173

Evolution 175

Eclipsed By Tradition 179

Church History 180

Camping 190

Unraveling Conversation 194

Leaving Church 196

Paint By Numbers 199

Old Journals 201

Label 203

Eclipsed by My Own Life 207

Golden Handcuffs 208

Harvest 211

Grounded 216

Almost 223

Coming into the Light 231

Epilogue 233

Acknowledgments 235

Author Biography 241

Notes 243

Introduction

I'm an astronaut.

In middle school, I watched the movie *The Right Stuff* a dozen times—and that's a serious two-VHS, three-plus hour kind of commitment that spans fifteen years of history about the space program. I went to Space Camp in Huntsville, Alabama, and its sophomore camp, Space Academy, the following year. I spent six months saving for a bomber jacket from Wilsons Leather at Oxmoor Mall to emulate the great Chuck Yeager, my test-pilot hero who was the first person to break the sound barrier in a plane. I dreamed of going to the Air Force Academy and had pictures of F-16 fighter planes in my young teenage bedroom peppered among my posters of Jon Bon Jovi and Cory Haim. My heart was set on being an astronaut. I dreamed of a life lifting off into the universe and living among the stars as I explored the Milky Way and all her planets. I was absolutely positive I would one day see the far side of the moon. Just certain of it.

That is, until I took algebra. Even with all the extra help my teacher Ms. Morgan gave me, I was struggling. She would lean over my shoulder, and her raspy smoker's voice would hint at what my next steps should be, but I'd still end up in tears, completely defeated. Math literally did not compute for me.

Same with science. I loved the idea of discovery and was curious about the physical and natural world, but I realized I was more enamored with its wonder. At that age, figuring everything out about what I'd seen, unearthed with such fascination, almost took the fun out of it for me. I realized I just wanted to gaze up at the stars and dream about the cosmic dance more than I wanted to dissect frogs or sort through the study of systems. All that time I'd spent imagining a life in the celestial spaces, and now I was grounded by the reality that, well, it just wasn't going to happen. Sure, I could have hired tutors and worked endlessly on equations and laws of constant composition, but I suppose I realized I just didn't want it badly enough. So, while the science-savvy students were taking chemistry and the math-minded kids were taking trigonometry, I was playing office aid and helping with the freshman chorus.

Eventually, I took those plane posters down from my wall and stopped telling people my leather jacket was in homage to a pilot many of them had never heard of. (That announcement was kind of awkward anyway, so that was probably for the best.) Still, I kept his autograph in a keepsake box and teed up that helluva long movie a time or two more. My days of hoping for a NASA career were behind me.

But I'm still an astronaut, and I've spent a long time out in space, looking for the far side of the moon.

I got here honestly. My intense connection to the cosmos never left me in all my Space Camp, bomber jacket early ambitions. I have always felt most held by God out in the open air. Nothing is hidden or well-known out in the great expanse. And I can't help but marvel at it all.

But.

I've spent long seasons out at the edge, looking back at how I thought life on Earth was supposed to be for me. I've hovered above the bustle of life, longing to engage in it all and hesitant to risk exposure. And I've lingered for seasons in the radio silence on the far side, when events, people, hurt, anxiety, and all the rest have sent me scrambling to hide where the noise of messy life can't get through.

Here's the thing. The majesty of the universe can seem preferable to the conversely majestic entanglement of people and life. When astronauts live in space for even just a short while, their muscles atrophy from working considerably less. When they leave the skies to re-engage with the literal weight of the world, they have to acclimate to what those of us down here have been steadily managing. It's the same when we allow ourselves to live in the clouds, detaching from the call of fully living. At the time, it can seem as though staying eclipsed might be far easier than re-engaging in the breakneck pace and inevitable pains of life earthside. But that is where our stories live. And along with the chaos, there is the joy and beauty and awe of us. When I came back into "radio contact," I had to hone the small voice within me. Through its cues, I began to strengthen the muscles of discernment and self-reliance, realize and face the forces that kept me sequestered. It was difficult at first, but I had stayed hidden for long enough. At some point, the idea of dimming down my own destiny to live in the shadows seemed more daunting than being fully known.

"Hurry, Mama!! We're not gonna make it!" urges the voice beside me. I have to almost lift my right hip off the worn-out gray upholstery of the truck's bench seat to give it gas. The handle to adjust the seat is broken, so any repositioning has to be done manually. Sweat is beading on my forehead and trailing down under the nose of my knock-off sunglasses. The two sets of cheeks to my right are flushed from both the hot August day and their apprehension over whether we'll get there on time. Their matching strawberry blonde ponytails jostle up and down as I careen down the road. I give my leg another stretch to punch the pedal, and the girls cheer me on as we pass a slower passenger before the two lanes merge to one.

Their chant of "Beat-that-car! Beat-that-car!" is both encouraging and insistent. They scan the sky for clues. Will we be too late? I clasp the shaky steering wheel and go in full tilt, grateful that the rocks ricocheted by the tires will go unnoticed on the sides of this old beater. Before I can even get the dashboard gear shift into park, the girls bolt out, open the front door of our friends' house, tear through the kitchen, and race to the back yard to where all the others are eagerly waiting.

I search through my cream canvas bag to grab the picnic blanket and safety gear the teachers had passed out to the kids before early release from school. I help my youngest get hers on and make sure the oldest is all set too. Check. All the adults are glued to their phones and giving updates from the tracking app, so we know when it's coming. One mom looks up and shouts, "Okay!! YES! It's about to start!!"

We turn our collective attention to the sky.

And it begins.

The moon slowly begins its slide across the circle of the sun, gradually swallowing up her brilliance with its shadow.

The kids are adjusting their rainbow paper and black polymer protectors, and the parents are snapping pictures of the moon's progression over earth's closest star. Our shadows are becoming sharper, outlined by the remaining sliver of the sun. The little crew of backyard kiddos cheers on the moon as it completes its coverage. The air is cooler yet electric with excitement. The sky is colored with a unique hue of darkness, unlike night. Everything about it is magical.

A total eclipse.

I feel a tear stream down my cheek and onto my lips and taste the salt from my skin. With my glasses in position, I strain to see past the visible veil of the sky. I'm mesmerized. And also, oddly sort of sad. It occurs to me that the awe of the eclipse phenomenon does not just arrest me but that there's also something very familiar about it all.

I go where I always go when I need answers: The Omniscient Presence of the Internet, Google. A click on Wikipedia tells me:

> "A solar eclipse occurs when a portion of the Earth is engulfed in a shadow cast by the Moon which fully or partially blocks sunlight . . . In a total eclipse, the disk of the Sun is fully obscured by the Moon. A solar eclipse happens when the moon gets in the way of the sun's light and casts its shadow on Earth. That means during the day, the moon moves over the sun and it gets dark."[1]

The word *eclipse* turns out to be revelatory. It's of Greek origin, its root word *ekleipen*, which means to *fail to appear* and *to leave out*.

Well then. That would explain that vaguely melancholic response I had when watching the phenomenon with my daughters.

Oh, how I have felt eclipsed.

Engulfed in the shadows. Swallowed up. Unseen.

I've let a number of things obstruct my true self from appearing on the scene: the need for approval, meeting expectations, traps of tradition, allegiance to addiction, past mistakes, present circumstances, future casting.

And so, instead of stepping into my own light, I just sort of started fading away. Sometimes the shadow I was in was intentionally cast in my direction so as to capture me whole. Other times, I intentionally slipped behind the moon until all but a paper-thin outline of me remained.

Sometimes I was overshadowed by expectations—both those I strived to meet and those I would never live up to. Then there's the pall of tradition that engulfed me and kept me busy polishing pretense to stay in its presence but yearning for the actual Light. And with that came the shadow of doubt that I found myself in as I hid behind a false faithfulness to save face. For a time, I stood in a silhouette of success that never felt earned, and other times I stood in the shadow of unrealized success I had so hoped for. I failed to appear for the work that I wanted to explore because I was too busy striving for goals at that "great job" I had that "people would die to have." Then there were the shadows of the past that I was constantly trying to stand in and live up to. It's hard to show up as your true self when you're working hard to be what you think everyone needs you to be. Of course, there was the shadow cast by the mountain of the moment I was in, with its list of to-dos piled so high that I forgot there was light out there at all. Instead of living, I was hurdle-jumping all day just to make it to the finish line with all the bars still standing. And to be sure, I've been swallowed up by the fear of what was on the other side of said mountain: tomorrow. I've eclipsed the present moment by catastrophizing about the future. Then there was the shadow of dusk when the drinking began, and the light dimmed with each sip, and I failed to appear in my own life, around my dinner table. At some points, my light was so faint it almost faded away altogether. I almost disappeared completely. I was almost totally eclipsed.

But here's some good news: Eclipses are temporary.

In the physical universe, the sun, the moon, and the Earth all have to directly line up for an eclipse to happen.

They don't get to choose their alignment, their cycles of eclipse. But we do.

And just like we can position ourselves to be in alignment with the shadow cast by whatever foreboding presence is in front of us, we can also just move.

All this to say, it's up to us.

For a while now, I've been on a consistent quest to discover the difference between who I was programmed to be, what I'm supposed to believe, and how I should behave, versus who I really am, what I truly believe, and how I want to live. Along the way I've learned some things:

I'm learning to say what I need without having a "me first" attitude.

I'm learning to look at myself in the mirror and find my own beauty because I see the beauty in everyone, not just the girls in the magazines.

I'm learning to say, "Oh, this shade that you're trying to throw is just not gonna work for me anymore."

I'm learning that accommodating doesn't always mean yielding and shrinking back my preferences just because I might be in a position to honor someone else's.

I'm learning to rock the boat when it needs to be rocked instead of swallowing back hard conversations to maintain smooth sailing.

I'm learning to appreciate smooth sailing instead of rocking the boat out of fear that it's going to sink one day.

I'm learning to toughen up without becoming calloused or cynical.

I'm slowly learning to lay down my defensive reactions because finding my voice doesn't have to mean protecting my rightness or ensuring someone completely understands everything about my response.

I'm learning when to extend the benefit of the doubt and when to call bullshit straight out of the gate.

I'm learning to communicate when I'm becoming frazzled because I know that the ability to spin too many plates does not define my worth. This means I'm learning to cut the meltdown off at the pass.

I'm learning that being all-in is better than checking out, no matter the situation.

I'm learning that certainty is the stranglehold of mystery.

I'm learning that just as I came into agreement with the lie that I am not enough, I can also break that agreement. And the lie has no say in the matter.

I'm learning that no one gets to decide who I am except for me.

Maybe you can relate to some of these. Maybe you have your own list of things you're learning. Maybe you've felt swallowed up by something or someone in your own life.

We as women can spend so much time orbiting around the things that take us away from ourselves just because their gravitational pull is so strong. We have to listen for that whisper that brings us back home, to the Light within us, to the Light that *is* us.

This isn't a book you have to read straight through in sequential order. Not if you don't want to. I want you to feel the freedom to jump to topics. Maybe it's a book you pick up to read in the early morning, taking in an essay a day, letting the thoughts roll around in your head and heart. Maybe it's something you read straight through in one sitting.

You'll meet some important players along the way:

The cute guy from my hometown who was my almost-college boyfriend and who is now my husband, Ben, who I sometimes call B.

My oldest daughter Celia, who is a slice of my soul and who is marked by curiosity. Answering her little girl questions about God made the wobbly wheels of my religion come off. And my youngest daughter Annie, the cutest little guru you ever did see who calls things like they are with words of compassionate candor.

You'll encounter me referring to myself by my maiden name, Mathis. You'll hear me talk about myself as a Hardin, my married name. You'll hear about my grandmothers, Grandmom Mathis and Grandmom Maddox, my friends, namely Katye and Lisa, my unnamed but incredible tribe of women, my mom and dad, known as Mama and Daddy, my brother Lewis, my therapist, and my hometown of Shelbyville, Kentucky.

You'll read about some of the different hats I wear: mama, wife, Realtor, Airbnb host, singer.

These are my people and places and things. This is my story. It's my hope that you'll find some of your own story here as well.

Eclipsed
by Approval

There is a story I used to tell myself on loop until it became a mantra, engulfing my soul. It was a sly introduction to the lifelong battle it would push me toward. It usually began as a suggestion and then spread like sourdough starter. And it was this: I AM NOT ENOUGH.

The subplot of this narrative was that if I could just gain enough affirmation in the form of 'atta girls' and accolades, I'd be worthy of approval.

I would be enough.

Looking back, I can see that approval was my first addiction. The desire built on itself and grew roots. Those roots branched off and planted their own trees, and then suddenly I was surrounded by a forest of approval rooted in insecurities developed and nurtured on ever-shifting soil. And still, it was never enough.

I think a lot of us have a version of this story resounding in our hearts, telling us we will never live up to so and so's high standards or meet the world's expectations or reach the ever-raising bar for what it means to be beautiful. I am not alone in this, and neither are you.

BODY

Becky had boobs. Like, full and actual breasts. They were glorious. Somehow during the summer between fourth and fifth grade, she must have gotten a magical potion poured on her chest that made her grow a perfect pair. Meanwhile, all I got to show up with on my first day of school was a Trapper Keeper from Rose's with a cute Labrador on it. I was less impressed with my carefully selected school supply after I saw Becky's impressive additions.

Not only did she get new knockers, she also got a bra to go with them. In fact, I started noticing telling outlines under the shirts of other girls in my grade. Did EVERYONE but me have one? I wanted a bra! I thought that if the world was so cruel as to deny me what goes into said bra, that didn't mean I couldn't at least have the coveted accessory.

When I brought my request before my mom, she was surprised. Looking back from my own mama perspective now, she must have really had to work hard not to giggle. I was as flat as the blackboard Mrs. Druin wrote our homework assignments on, so it didn't stand to reason that I needed any kind of undergarment support to hold up my nothingness. To her credit, Mom took me to JCPenney shortly after I entered my plea, and we went shopping for a training bra.

It was a white satin confection with a pink bow in the middle along the front seam. I didn't even care that the straps were itchy and that the whole thing was uncomfortable. I was in the club! The tricky part was that I had literally nothing to hold this holster in place, so as I moved around, my newly procured bra was in a constant state of migration up and down my featureless torso. There were no hills to ride, no valleys in which to cling to. I found myself adjusting it all the time. The band wasn't tight enough to stay in place, and there was nothing but sprouting buds in the cup. When I moved my body, the bra wiggled up toward my armpits.

Determined to keep wearing it, I invented the "pull-down." I tied a string around the middle of my bra at the signature pink bow and ran it under my shirt and into my jeans pocket. The plan was that if (read when) the bra rode up, I could pull down on the string with my hand in my pocket (because *inconspicuous*, of course) to readjust. Clever as I was, it wasn't what I'd call a smashing success. After a full day of making adjustments that were even more awkward with my created contraption, I threw in the towel.

Or, in this case, the bra.

It was clear that my time had not yet come, and so I abandoned Project Bra. The bra was relegated to the top drawer of my white wicker dresser for almost a year before I gave it another try. Still, I never did fill it out like Becky.

I'm still a little mad about it. Dangit, Becky.

While I wasn't thrilled that there was barely any delineation between my chest and my stomach, the fact that I was one of the last girls in school to start my period was cool enough by me. I was kinda grossed out by the whole thing and not in any hurry to cross the menstrual threshold. I did sort of want to cross the threshold into . . . I don't think I was dumb enough to say "womanhood," but maybe just to join the rest of the crew on the other side of the menstrual rite of passage from little girlhood.

But menses waits for no one.

It happened in school. I remember having a distinct feeling of knowing that I was starting pretty much the actual moment I did, and I was grateful I had dodged the dread of discovering it from finding it on my pants along with the rest of the eighth grade. Thank you, Blessed Lord, that fellow classmate Joanna Pridemore was in the hall the exact moment I needed her. She was prepared with period provisions in her backpack and met me in the girls' bathroom behind the auditorium. She stood outside the stall door and guided me through the whole process of peeling the back off the sticky side of the maxi pad and where exactly to put it on my underwear. And talk about true friendship: she then did a pants check to make sure I didn't look like I was walking around with a crotch diaper in my Jordache jeans. I had seen the ads in *Teen* magazine of a ballerina walking out of the door with the thought bubble above her head, "Do you think they'll notice?"

My guess from the bulge between my legs: Yes. Yes, they will notice. Like the minute you walk in late to Mr. Matthews' social studies class. They. Will. Notice.

Thank God for the tampon. Really. And thank you Tampax, for assuring us that if we use your more unobtrusive product, we will still be virgins. I mean, I wasn't near ready to lose my virginity anyway, but I sure didn't want to give it to a cardboard applicator and uncomfortable squared-off chunk of cotton with a cord coming out of it. Especially with no candlelight or background music like my older cousin said it would go down.

Boobs weren't the only item I was obsessing over in my high school years. Teen magazines were the Gospel for Girls, as far as I was concerned. I studied them with the fervor of a teen theologian, ever searching for enlightenment on trends, make-up how-tos, and fitness tips. I wasn't the only acolyte; there was a whole congregation of us, my friends and I, who thought of 'that time of the month' as when our latest teen tomes would arrive in magazine form in our mailboxes. And those magazines put us on alert for all the unattractive things we need to be on the lookout for and all the examples of who we should try to be.

First on the teen magazine most wanted list of offenders were pimples. Acne became a new enemy, an evil foe who had exquisitely horrible timing, rising to the surface just in time for a social outing or date with a new crush. I needed ammunition to fight this villain. My first bottle of Sea Breeze (raise your hand if you know. Raise your hand again if you can memory-smell that aqua blue astringent goodness right now) was a gift from my grandmother, a not-so-subtle nod to the missteps of my complexion. I saturated a handful of cotton balls with the promising astringent. This potion was supposed to make my face feel tingly. Which it did—until it felt like fiery lava. But I took this as a promising sign that the product was working extra hard for me. Surely the extra applications would speed up this bane of puberty, and surely my skin would be clear by Friday night's football game. Being desperate, even though it was near painful, I persisted. Instead of a blemish-free face, I ended up with pimples plus dry patches around said pimples as a result of the assault on my skin.

If I couldn't manage to zap all of my zits, I would up my hair game. And by up, I mean go big. This would also take some work. My fine nondescript brown strands fell flat around my face, and no amount of Finesse mousse in my perm ever did the trick of creating that full look past the two-hour mark. But I did eventually master a strong bang game. I stood in our butter yellow bathroom, my creative studio for creating hair magic. It was a complex, multi-step process, which involved tightly curling my bangs under and then sculpting the left side up an inch high. I would brush and spray this section of bangs into a curling peak, a crest of a wave to reign over the rest of my permed mane. Central to this configuration was copious amounts of Final Net, cementing everything in place. I then created side wings between my temple and the top of my ear by catching some otherwise fraying strands between my fingers, cascading them out to the side, and shooting them with half a dozen targeted pumps of hair spray. From the front, everything was spread tall and wide like I'd been electrocuted, and from the back, my limp locks lay draggling behind the facade all my effort had managed.

That's how I spent so much of my time as I was becoming a young woman. Elaborate fronts of padded bras and pancake makeup over zits and chemically constructed lion's mane of hair, while the real me straggled along, caught in the wake of faux. And that wasn't the only frontage I was hiding behind. I learned early on to project confidence I didn't

There was the fiction of what was outward-facing, and then there was what was really going on behind.

have. I slapped on a brave face over deep fears. I slathered on nonchalance when my heart was breaking. There was the fiction of what was outward-facing, and then there was what was really going on behind.

There's a phrase in the military and law enforcement: I've got your six. It's what people in arms will call out to one another, committing to protect and defend where it can be hard to see. It speaks to the truth that one of our most vulnerable places is not what we've got in front of us. It's what's behind us that can take us down. We shine light on what we want to be seen and leave the insecurities and doubts and panic back there in the eclipse of our public shadow. But that's where the personal monsters dwell. And they whisper things like, "Only show what you've got covered. But we know what's ugly and lacking and hidden behind."

I even forgot at times that there was a backside, an underneath, to all I was projecting. Just like the woeful girl who comes wandering out of the bathroom with the back of her dress tucked in her underwear and a streamer of toilet paper trailing from her heel, I was often so focused on projecting a fabricated fluorescence that I'd forget to check my own six, to acknowledge and see where the tenderest parts of myself could lay exposed.

It made the news a few years ago. In the heat of an intense soccer match between two opposing women's teams, a player felt her hijab, the religious veil worn by Muslim women in the presence of men outside of family, begin to slip. Members of the opposing team saw her stop and begin to reach for her hijab. And in a moment of spectacular humanity, they surrounded her and used their bodies to create privacy for her. It didn't matter if they understood or agreed with her reasons for wearing the hijab. It didn't matter that she was on another team. What mattered in that moment was that they had her six. They were proactive in showing up for her, protecting her where she would feel exposed, demonstrating that compassion and sheltering transcend competition between women, whether on the soccer field, in the dating game, in the boardroom, or in the mommy gaggle.

As women, we've got to check each other's six. And that means we have to be trusted with what we find there. We have to exercise love for our fellow woman by covering her back when the proverbial hem of her dress is anchored in the waistband of her panties. And we need to show up as a team player for ourselves. There are so many of us who have allowed only the veneer of ourselves to be seen. We pad the truth of who we really are. We dose ourselves in astringent words about our worth just because we have blemishes on our souls. We try to hide behind the halo of heavily sprayed hair, inflating our profiles. We've got to trust that what's behind all of that is more beautiful, more true, and more real. It's the best thing we could bring into the light.

CLEAN KITCHEN

I love mopping.

I get that it's weird, but let me explain.

It's not the actual act of it, but the immediate return on my investment of a few minutes of swishing the lemon-scented water across the floor. One second my floor is dirty, splattered with spilled drinks, patterned with footprints from rainy shoes, and peppered with crumbs that fell and found themselves smashed onto the hardwood. We repurposed an old basketball gym floor on the main level of our house, and the blonde planks highlight almost every one of our everyday messes. And believe me, there are plenty of them. When I finally tire of that mysterious sticky spot squeaking under my flip flops, I'll grab the mop from our garage and glide it back and forth until—voila!—a clean floor. Even the girls don't mind mopping. My daughter Annie says it's her favorite chore because "it's so satisfying."

The truth is, I love a neat house in general. It doesn't have to be spotless. I'm cool if you can write your initials in the dust across my coffee table, but I want the books on said table to be nicely arranged. My kitchen island seems like the gigantic catch-all in our house—school papers, real estate folders, water bottles, and keys. When the house is tidy, or at the very least the island is clear, I've got a sense of control over things. When my physical space is decluttered, I can think more clearly and create more freely. Clean lines give me a sense of security, albeit as temporal as the time between messes. it's my Jedi mind trick for feeling like I'm put together more than I am. For both reasonable and ridiculous outcomes, I scurry and straighten my way toward a sense of sanctity.

Because I simply can't manage it all by myself (and because close to the top of my list of Ways to Raise My Daughters to Be Powerful doesn't include making them entitled divas), the girls have daily chores around here too. And for some reason, in the middle of an average day during a typical conversation with a friend, I had an overwhelming need to announce this fact.

My friend Lisa and I ran into each other. She's a mom to three boys, and she was talking about having to deep clean their house in preparation for company. Instead of being interested in her and asking about their upcoming visit, I interjected with, "We have the girls clean the kitchen."

Umm. She didn't ask who cleaned our kitchen.

Also, I don't really care who cleans theirs.

And what in the actual world prompted me to make that announcement? My kitchen might be clean, but my heart? Nope. Gross.

Being gracious, she gave me a pass on being an asshole, and we continued our conversation with talk about our summers.

A few days later, I sent her a message. We have a friendship that is nurtured and sustained through Marco Polo. (The app. Not the explorer.) It's where we can reach out to each other with quick videos about what's going on in our days. And as it turns out, it's a handy place to send an apology. I told her I was so sorry that I made my comment about having my girls clean right in the middle of her telling me about the stress of getting her place ready for company. I told her that I had spent time thinking through why I commented in the first place. Because she's a vault-safe place to land, here's what I confessed:

Things weren't going so great in a particular area of my parenting world. And because I was feeling so rotten about that specific area of my mothering, I projected something that I *was* proud of. That my kids clean the kitchen. That they have chores.

Isn't that just so ridiculous? But that was my why.

After I cracked open that door, I decided to just go ahead and fling it wide open. I got in my car and Marcoed Lisa, driving while I processed with her. I traced a personal history to Lisa of other times I'd hung my hat on some point of pride and how it was to typically distract people from the otherwise glaringly obvious shortcomings of my actual life.

Like when I needed to make sure the women in my moms' group knew I had natural childbirth, breastfed for a year, and am raising my girls on a very healthy diet. Quinoa, anyone? Then maybe my mom peers would think I was strong, resilient, and generally awesome and then not see me struggling to balance working and mom-ing.

Or sometimes it's keeping up the completely annoying family practice I'd learned in childhood to justify everything I put into my mouth by making sure you knew I'd be running an extra mile after the forbidden cupcake or caloric treat. I can feel this need to reassure my eating audience (and myself) that I have a plan of action to rid myself of any splurge-induced gain. As if you somehow cared enough to be running calorie estimates on me. See how disciplined (and irritating) I am?

I've done it when talking about the beautiful loft we lived in, making sure you know that we were just as happy as when we lived in the eleven-hundred square foot cottage we had before. (In other words, I'm not attached to things. This is sneaky pride that sounds like humility. You gotta be on the lookout for this one with careful attention.)

If I show you my wins, you may not see my losses. If I can mitigate you thinking I'm getting all boasty or braggy, then you might just like me better. If I can cover my deficits with my sufficiency, then maybe you'll think me a winner. And if you don't mind, could you just focus on those wins? Thank you very much.

Even though I've done a lot of work on my heart, even though I would have said I'd overcome this need to measure up constantly, I didn't realize until that conversation just how much pride still lurks, ready to spring out at the latest provocation. And here's the thing about pride: it's a masquerade for the need for approval. It convinces us that we better flaunt and enhance what we've got because if someone could see our net value, we wouldn't be enough with all our debits and credits. So, we let pride take out the mortgage on our souls and use that to face the world. These days I tend to let my flaws hang out, but things like the need for approval that are so deeply embedded into our hearts die a hard, slow death. Lisa says it's like working out a splinter. I love that analogy. And she gets the tweezers out and helps me as I wince my way through the process.

> **If I can cover my deficits with my sufficiency, then maybe you'll think me a winner. And if you don't mind, could you just focus on those wins?**

(Sidebar: After this beautiful and vulnerable conversation, I arrived back home a little lighter, having laid down some of my burdens. And when I walked through the front door, my kitchen was an absolute disaster. I video-captured the shit storm state of it all and sent it to Lisa, commenting, "Turns out I'm not even winning on this front." Life will humble your pride and expose your need for approval every time, friend. Every. Time.)

BINGE

Everyone had gone to bed. I couldn't sleep for the nagging voices of anxiety, though I didn't know them as anything other than my inability to pull myself together back then. I jolted out of bed with absolute terror. I could not breathe. I was panicked and I wanted a hit of something that would make me feel better. At this time in my life, I sported a coping mechanism for all things anxiety-related: smoking.

My cigarette usage was keeping pace with the Marlboro man himself, and it would have been my go-to activity in this midnight waking, but I couldn't smoke in the house where I was staying, and I didn't want to trip the alarm on my way out the door. That left me the option of food, and I strategically tiptoed down the hardwood halls to not hit a creaking plank.

Once my feet landed on the linoleum floor of the kitchen, I darted toward the refrigerator for leftover fried fish. I grabbed a handful of cookies from the covered plate on the counter and snuck behind the small pantry door. I shoveled the cold fish and chocolatey cookies into my mouth like a hungry hippo. The combination of salty and sweet shot dopamine through my pain. I plowed through the pantry, quietly opening various packages and getting just enough to add to my binge buffet but not enough for the next person to notice the missing treats. The resulting rush was hitting hard enough to knock me over.

Moments after I'd smashed through the snacks, I lay in a fetal position, thinking that if I could just squeeze my eyes shut and my body tight, I could make the agony go away. But it was still there, and getting worse. I had harmed my body again. I would pay penance come tomorrow when I'd force myself to work out, pushing myself harder, faster, longer, all to undo this night's continued pattern of personal punishment.

The odd thing was, I wasn't sure what I was punishing myself for. The food was filling a hole in my heart, but I didn't know what caused the hole in the first place. I assumed it had something to do with sin. So I prayed for better eating habits and to be righteous and holy, and for forgiveness of the things I'd done that weren't either. If ever a thought did rise up that pointed to a wound that needed tending, I didn't have much in my toolbox back then other than the idea of believing bad things away. But that wasn't working much anymore.

I did not live inside of myself during those dark days. There was no mind-body-spirit connection. My body was a source of shame for me. It was never beautiful enough or thin enough or pure enough or strong enough or clear-skinned enough or big-boobed enough. Even after compliments to the contrary. Even after I lost the weight. Even after I went on Accutane as an adult and my skin cleared up. Even after my A cups got surgically upsized to a full C. Still, I found things to reject. I thought my once high and tight tush was shrinking. My arms not toned enough. My hair still boring.

The result? I didn't care for my body. Instead, I hovered over this subpar shape I was confined to live in with disdain and disgust and disrespect. I convinced myself that what I saw as my shortcomings meant that there was no way a critical world could ever approve of me.

> **I convinced myself that what I saw as my shortcomings meant that there was no way a critical world could ever approve of me.**

And so, I did not approve of myself. In practice, I punished myself.

Of course, I didn't see it that way at the time. I didn't see midnight raids to the pantry as a form of punishment for not meeting the world's criteria. I didn't see the cigarettes I breathed or, later, the alcohol I made my daily lover as any kind of penance for my lack.

But it was. And once I realized what I was doing and why, I thought I was the only one.

Turns out, I'm not the only one.

So many women. So many of us do this to ourselves. In our own ways, in our own means, for our own reasons. We raid whatever pantry is available: achievement, shopping, activities, all manner of more, more, more, all while it bleeds us dry. We have even fooled ourselves at times to call it 'self-care.' But our energy, bank account, and calendar are bleeding out, and we still feel like we're falling short.

It's taken some time, but I've learned to take much better care of myself. To give myself what I need from a place of lovingkindness. I've learned to exchange the hair shirt of self-condemnation that left me itching to get out of my own skin for a garment made of soul-deep self-compassion. I realize now that it's what I was starving for all along.

BETRAYAL

I asked my counselor about the subject of betrayal. Her answer reminded me that betrayal isn't just major issues like infidelity that we typically think of when we hear the word. Instead, it's an ongoing assessment of the question, "Can I count on you to be there when I need you?" She said it could be as big as adultery or as small as not remembering to bring home milk. She assured me that we're all going to fall short but, if we do a good repair with our partner, we teach them that emotionally we are trustworthy. We show them we will do our best to mend things when we blow it. We won't just leave them out to dry when we fall short.

That's betrayal in the context of a relationship, and that was a natural way to answer the question I had posed. But then it made me think about the other primary relationship in my life, the relationship that can also experience the heartache and challenge of betrayal: the relationship with myself. Am I there for myself when I need to be able to count on *me*?

What happens when the answer is no?

I think about how often I have betrayed myself for a paramour of approval. How often I have allowed my true self to be eclipsed by becoming what I thought someone expected me to be.

How many times have I responded with one answer when I really thought another?

How frequently have I gone along with something when my BS alarm was sounding because I did not want to rock the boat?

How many times have I nodded, "Yes" when I really thought, "No?"

In those circumstances, it seemed more important to me that the person on the other side of the conversation walked away pleased with my response, even if my inner dialogue was conflicted.

And then I got to wondering, what is the root of that self-betrayal? I concluded that I must value the other person above the value I place on myself. Not in the healthy way that I put others before me. No—it stems from the belief that *I don't matter as much as they do.*

When faced with a decision or conversation, I tempered my reaction, emotion, thought, or idea to let the other person have their way. Here's the result of trying to be the flexible one, the pleasing one, the accommodating one: I've been predictably unfaithful to myself when I wanted someone to like me. When I wanted their approval. I have times I'll buck an unjust system or own my opinion; but when my need for approval has outpaced my relationship with myself, I take on a mistress again, the one that whispers that my silence or acquiescence just might, perhaps, make me worthy. I've gone to great lengths to win favor, making another's opinion of me the sum of my net worth.

Why doesn't it register that when I start to dim, that's when it's time to duck out of that crowd altogether until I can learn to stand on my own two feet? (Hint . . . those are warning signs.)

Sometimes, my confidence is on fire. I can walk into a meeting or on stage feeling prepped, poised, and positioned to succeed.

Other times, I can stiffen, stumble, and stammer through situations like someone who's been held as a recluse, unaware of social and cultural expectations.

Am I the only one? My guess is that I'm not alone.

We're taught to adapt and flex to accommodate others at the expense of being true to ourselves. I mean, it's kind of the world system I grew up in. I love all the "Be Yourself" messaging kids are getting these days, but back in my day it was, "Be a good girl."

Like little chameleons, we learned to

Please our parents.
Please our peers.
Please our teachers.
Please our boss.
Please our partner.
Please the crowd.

And in the pleasing, so many of us are taught to counterfeit our authenticity for the sake of making others feel good about who they are or what they are doing. Think about some of the messages we get, from faking smiles to faking orgasms. We're programmed on how to make a great first impression, how to thrill our partners in the sheets, and even *How to Win Friends and Influence People*.[2]

So many of us are taught to counterfeit our authenticity for the sake of making others feel good about who they are or what they are doing.

For far too long, I have been easily swayed by the winds of opinion. My husband Ben's opinion used to top the list, and I was programmed to submit to my husband through all kinds of faith language. Thankfully, as we've broken free from some of those misunderstood doctrines, it has mattered less. Don't get me wrong, his opinion still counts and is important to me because I value him deeply, but not in a defining way that leaves me sculpting myself to fit his mold. And we both like it better that way. As it turns out, he loves me for *me*. Who would've thought? And that means I don't have to fake anything when it comes to Ben, which you can interpret however you like.

I glance back at the trail of treason I committed against myself.

Self, can I count on you to be there when I need you?

Not when I stayed in that toxic marriage for too long because good Christian girls don't get divorced.
Not when I accepted the promotion instead of giving my two weeks' notice.
Not when I let that guy on my sales team make that inappropriate comment while I held my tongue and nervously tried to laugh it off.

What about those times when I betrayed myself even when no one else was looking?

When I pounded potato chips instead of going for a walk.
When I poured that next drink though I knew it was killing me.
When I put off writing a book for another year because next year might make more sense.
Or when I stay up late scrolling when my body is begging for rest. Or compare myself to others. Or miss the Now moment for catastrophizing about the Next moment.

It shatters my soul when I think about how often my heart, or my convictions, have been the casualty of friendly fire.

Self-love in the form of faithfulness took me a while to learn. I had to start with the small stuff. Like drawing my weary body a bath to tend to my sore muscles. Or giving myself more rest or good food when I needed it. I worked my way up to the bigger things as I began to trust myself with the smaller ones.

The hardest lessons are the ones that take me the longest to learn. But once I get it, it grows roots. Finally, I understand. I am worthy of fidelity to myself. When I cheat *on* myself, I *cheat* myself. I have finally divorced the toxic partner of duplicity and made a lifelong vow to authenticity, whatever the cost. Because I deserve nothing less than the wholehearted love of my soul.

HOME INSPECTION

The rooms were bright and airy, with plenty of natural light pouring in through the large windows. The fresh gray paint on the kitchen walls looked crisp against the wood-grain cabinets adorned with quirky knobs. The gorgeous great room boasted vaulted ceilings and a quaint fireplace—the perfect spot to entertain or to play family games on Sunday afternoons in front of the fire. And the backyard was to die for. Sprawling with the possibility of raised gardens and a fire pit for gathering with friends. It looked just perfect! It all just seemed too good to be true.

I've been a Realtor for several years now. With the work Ben and I do in real estate investment and rehab, along with our Airbnb side hustles, it was inevitable that I would end up as your friendly neighborhood agent. Whenever my clients make an offer on a house, the next step in their buying process is to order a home inspection. In the case of the home I just described, we expected a report with maybe a few items to address, but neither the soon-to-be owners nor myself had much concern.

I was surprised to get a phone call from the inspector the day following his visit. Typically, he just shoots over the report with pictures and descriptions of any repairs needed, getting us one step closer to closing day. I could tell from his greeting that he was not calling with good news.

"Well, Melinda, the house is really charming, but when I took a good look, there are a lot of issues. There's evidence of mold in the basement, some structural issues with the chimney, wiring that's not up to code, and the water heater is on its last leg. That's just for starters. It's a long report, and I'll send it over. Basically, the house *looks* great at first glance, but when you look closer, it's a mess. And it's going to take a lot of work to get things right."

My buyers were both surprised and crushed to learn this. They were smitten with the charm of what they thought would be their next family home and had already allowed themselves to mentally move in. One asked, "How could it look that great on the outside, but have so many problems we didn't even notice?"

Instead of requesting the seller make the necessary repairs, they were too overwhelmed with the catalog of factors and ultimately decided to rescind their offer. With blighted hope, we regrouped and restarted their home search.

———

When I scroll social media, I get the sense that many of us are like that home—hiding our flaws behind the walls of filters so that people see only our best portrayals. We slap on a smile like a fresh coat of paint and hope no one notices the cracks in our walls. We project a very buttoned-up, polished, and sometimes completely made-up persona so everyone gets the sense that we're doing just fine, all the while hoping they "like" us.

This image management can prove exhausting as we negotiate the imposing identities of our true selves and the ones we've electronically altered to showcase to the world. All the peacocking feels disingenuous.

I was scrolling through Instagram the other day and landed on a picture of a college-aged girl our family knows. She was carefully positioned for the camera in her thong bikini, blown-out hair, and on-point makeup. Her caption was something about studying for finals.

As if I was falling for that.

Her caption could have read: "Please validate me. I'd love some 'gorgeous' comments and, of course, send over some fire emojis." At first, it made me shake my head with a grin at how obvious she was being. And then it made me sad; sad that this lovely person felt the need to pose, posture, and post this way, a land grab for some self-esteem acreage. And then I had to let a wave of conviction wash over me because *I've* been guilty of this. A lot of my contemporaries have been guilty of the very same thing, minus the thong bikini. Think about some of the glow-up features of our phone and its apps that let us soften our look, fade out the wrinkles, and define our cheekbones. And then there are our captions, declaring simple mantras for complex seasons and relationships in life. Here are some favorites:

"Twenty years together, and it's always been bliss!" I'm calling BS. If it's only bliss, then someone is not telling the truth. (I thought about posting an anniversary pic of Ben and me last year that read: "Fifteen years together. Twelve great ones. Three that nearly killed us.")

Those First Day of School pics where the mom is lamenting that her beaming babes in the picture will be away from her for so many hours. Never mentioned is the meltdown just before she snapped the photo, or the fact that she's secretly cheering inside to have those moments to herself.

During the peak of the pandemic, one of my best girlfriends shared a social profile for me to follow. She said the person had some cool mom tips for quarantine. My friend failed to mention that this mom practically had a cape and superpowers. I hopped on and was hooked on over-the-top, impressive mom moves for about thirty minutes until I could no longer take it. Does she have a staff? An in-house monogrammer? A chef? Was she an event planner in her working life? Child stylist? General one-upper? I had to unfollow her the very same day. When my girlfriend asked me if I liked any of her ideas, my response was, "Sure, they all looked great. But I felt too bad about myself as a person after I scrolled through her feed, so I just gave up on trying to pull off any of her post ideas on how to get your family to connect through crafting, gourmet meals, or photo shoots. We turned off our phones and watched an entire season of Stranger Things instead."

And hey, about that word 'feed' that we use to describe our social media posts. Let's think about that. When you have someone over for dinner, you don't serve them leftovers or the fuzzy pasta you forgot to throw out. You likely make some effort to entertain them, possibly even wow them. Same with social media. You're just putting out your best for display. And so is everyone else. That doesn't mean they don't have that same reek in their bins or stink in their storyline. Instead of wrapping our stories in pretense, let's stop participating in the sham of it all. I'm not saying we just serve up our moldy moments, but we could all use a scoop of real life on our plates. A potluck of all the flavors of our lives.

That's probably why I love "As-Is" home listings as a Realtor. It's an announcement to potential buyers that they can anticipate some problems and that the seller is not going to do anything to fix them for you. It's forthcoming, and I find that refreshing. I've come to call these homes "take it or leave it listings." I wonder what social media would be like if we were honest about being "As-Is." What if we could start relationships without the filters, knowing that we're all fixer-uppers? What if our listings about ourselves included an understanding of 'take it or leave it?' My guess is that we just might find the places our souls could call home with the people who truly want to be there with us.

I'm not saying we just serve up our moldy moments, but we could all use a scoop of real life on our plates. A potluck of all the flavors of our lives.

PAPER CUTS

It usually starts with something like pizza toppings. Sure, you'd love a slice of thin-crust veggie (hold the olives), but you'd be happy to have deep dish pepperoni and banana peppers. It's just lunch, after all. You can be easy breezy. And, sure, you're really in the mood for a romantic comedy, but you'll concede and roll with it when he suggests a shoot-em-up. You'll still get the buttery popcorn and peanut M&Ms, and those splurges alone will make it worth sitting through the sequel you can't tell apart from the original.

Further down the road, he suggests a vacation in a big city when you'd really prefer a little cabin in the woods, but it's cool. You can take all the action. Your respite can wait, and it's vital that his needs are met too. Plus, he'd for sure go the outdoorsy route if you mentioned it, but why not just accommodate?

And so it goes. From pizza toppings to paint colors to property purchases. Out of a desire to be the go-with-the-flow girlfriend, and later wife, I obliged Ben's preferences along the way. I did this with most people over the years, but it was different with Ben because he was my place, where I was supposed to be completely me.

The problem was the pedestal we placed each other on. Our road to romance has been . . . eventful. We had spied each other years before in a crowded church congregation. We had shared a powerful friendship, and the kind of 'almost' made for the big screen. I'd gone on to marry someone else. Through twists, turns, and an eventual stroke of serendipity, Ben and I were now free to be together, finally. But the years between wanting to be together and actually getting together gave our minds plenty of time to paint the perfect picture of what life as one would be like.

A natural evolution of being overly accommodating is eventually forfeiting your own preferences altogether. And an understandable consequence of consistently sidestepping your own desires is resentment. It's important to note here that Ben neither requested nor required my problematic practices. I suppose I moved along in this way to maintain good standing with his idea of me versus standing firm as the actual me. But the cost of disengaging from my desires was higher than my esteemed position upon his pedestal. I didn't want to be controversial in our conversations, so I obliged most of his ideas and plans pretty readily.

A strange thing happens when you don't tell your truth directly: The honesty of your pain begins to scratch tiny slices in your heart, like paper cuts. And before you know it, you forget what your truth is. If I gave Ben the answer he wanted in hopes of pleasing him, I'd find myself discontent. It was a discontent of my own doing, a scenario I had constructed. I did it by giving an enthusiastic "Yes!" when I didn't mean it, and once we started on that road of mild regret, I'd nitpick every small thing, my unconstituted bitchiness mismatched with my affirming original answer.

"Oh, the tangled web we weave" in hopes of approval. And to belong. And oh, how I hoped for Ben's approval. And how I longed to belong with him.

I think it was the unheard voice inside me that nudged me toward a drink. And then another. When you've got a field of paper cuts on the tender contours of your heart, wine seems just the thing to disinfect the throb. My girl, Merlot and I would huddle at the table and invite Inner Voice. We would secretly dialogue about what we really wanted but wouldn't say aloud. And by the time Ben got home, we were ready to rumble. Not with over-the-top gestures. But with passive insinuations of our unhappiness. Merlot and Inner Voice and me, we'd talk incessantly at a confused Ben, thinking that if we just filled up the room with enough words, then maybe he would figure out what we

> A strange thing happens when you don't tell your truth directly: The honesty of your pain begins to scratch tiny slices in your heart, like paper cuts. And before you know it, you forget what your truth is.

were really thinking. After all, we were dropping passive-aggressive clues all over the floor. Shouldn't he pick up on at least one of them? After me and Inner Voice and our wine were finished making a mess of the night, we'd promise to do better tomorrow.

Here's something I learned from those late-night pity covens: I couldn't maintain my pedestal position with half truth-telling and booze-induced belligerence. It's funny how I still told myself that it would be harder to tell my whole truth. To be all the way me. But who was the authentic voice in this situation? The one telling me to withhold my truth? The one telling me to come clean?

I had spent so many chapters of my life people-pleasing and keeping up the pace of pretense that I wasn't sure I knew. And the me that I could access after a few sips of my daily spirit selection seemed too sad to bring to the surface. Also, she was pissed. At herself. At her husband, who plowed through her unrequited requests because she didn't know how to communicate them. At everyone who expected something from her that she didn't have the energy to give. She had just enough reserves left to feebly pick up that bottle, pour, and fade away.

And here's another thing I learned about this crazy pedestal tightwire situation. I likewise put Ben on a pedestal and had expectations of how he was supposed to maintain that precarious perch. Don't get me wrong, B is my person. He's amazing, intriguing, and passionate. And . . . he's human. He's had times when his missteps made him lose his balance, he came crashing down, and we've narrowly escaped the casualty of our marriage. I flinch a bit whenever I hear someone talking about their marriage in knight-in-shining-armor kind of language. Nobody can keep on a knight's armor forever. First, it weathers a few chinks. Inevitably, at some point, the helmet has to come off to breathe, and the protective metal rusts. If we try to keep our partners at the top of an idealistic column or mounted on a chivalrous steed, there's going to be an even bigger mess when life, humanity, and circumstance come crashing down. And really, it's bound to happen in some sense or another.

In our marriage, I have had to learn to trust that it is okay to be a self truth-teller. A self truth-teller is different from your run-of-the-mill reliable fact dispenser. I'm honest when it comes to taxes, recounting social conversations, and business deals. I'd pat myself on the back all day long on those kinds of veracity. But it didn't dawn on me for a long time, not until the pedestal I'd perched on collapsed through innuendos and late-night crying jags and critical needle jabs at Ben, that I was a liar. A storyteller, telling the narrative I hoped he wanted. I remember when I was growing up, instead of being asked if someone was lying, the question would be posed as, "Are you telling me a story?" The root question, when you peel back the softer language, is, "Are you lying to me?" And sometimes I was telling a story, sometimes I was lying. All in good intention but lying just the same. Lying to be accommodating and kind and thoughtful and selfless.

And on the other side of that well-intended lie was the sludge of resentment in the pipes of my heart. A flash fire of anger that burst like a crazed torch when I careened down the tunnels of my soul. It's no wonder, because the viper's nest of resentment is built of lies. It's built of the stuff that remains when we don't own our preferences, when we don't ask for what we need, when we try to back our way into getting our wants and desires met. And just like we'd expect, a viper's nest is made to incubate all manner of poison.

I've had to learn to speak up before I find myself lashing out. Not through the muffled filter of my girl, Merlot. Not at the prompting of my Inner Voice, who then leaves me stammering for words. But just me. My voice, the one that resonates with honesty. I thought I was keeping power on the pedestal. As it turns out, the ground floor truth is the steadier place to be. And it's the only place from which we can build a foundation.

Eclipsed by Emotion

M ercurial. Feelings are mercurial. This was my mom's reminder to my younger self when I was all up in and overcome by my feelings.

When she first said it, I didn't know what she meant. I'm sure I nodded in agreement and slipped down to the bookshelf for the Dictionary to find out. Because there was no Google, and no way was she ever going to feed me what I could fend for myself.

She was basically telling me that my feelings could change quickly and without prediction, so I shouldn't put too much stock in them. As much as I may have felt dismissed as a teenage girl, her words have been my stake in steady ground when my feelings are floundering. Hang on heart; there could be a shift soon.

It doesn't mean you discount your feelings. It means you don't let them lord over you like they are cemented because you know they can be temporary. Then you can remain at the vantage point to see the full scope of your sensations and get a gauge from there. But the sum of them can shift your position for a long stay behind the sun, or you can peek behind it several times a day.

EMBODIMENT

Growing up in conservative Christian evangelicalism, I learned early on to detach from my body. It was a source of shame for all its desires. The result was disembodiment.

Exploring the Mind Body Spirit connection was encouraged by my yoga teacher but warned against by those close to me. It was "New Age-y," and I needed to be careful. Still, I was curious. In that chapter of my life, I made most of my choices driven by what I thought was my spirit, but really religion was steering the wheel. My mind would interrupt my spirit with pesky questions that I tried to quiet for many years. Having latched onto the doctrine of the purity culture movement, my body was a tricky thing, always at the ready to betray me and my morals. In addition to always trying to apologize for and hide certain aspects of my body, I had subscribed to the message that girls should look a certain way, stay a certain weight, and be a certain shape. I went to great lengths to pursue this elusive perfection. But it was also made very clear to me that my body was a source of lust, so it was my responsibility to cover up as much of it as possible so as not to be a stumbling block. I remember the teachings of what my body meant in marriage as well. Apparently, it still wasn't really mine. It was there to serve my husband's needs at his will and whim, and to keep him committed to our covenant by keeping him satisfied in the marital bed. In the wake of all these messages, I detached from my body as much as possible, becoming alienated from my soul's home. Essentially, I moved out of it.

As it turns out, as much as we might want to think of our physical existence as separate from our emotional existence, it's just not true. We're connected—mind, body, and soul—and when we detach from one of these expressions, it costs us in the others.

In my late twenties, I studied for a master's degree in Holistic Wellness. As you might imagine, there was a lot of curricula around integrating all the individual parts of ourselves to represent a whole. My mind understood this. My spirit was a little bit afraid of it. And my body was outside of the big picture but still reaping the benefits of my learning. As the months of study went on, I began to hover over my body a little more closely. Instead of looking at her from way up high with punitive posture every time she ate too much, I started wondering what it might be like if I cared for her a little more gently. In my yoga and Pilates practice, I would hear cues like, "Check in with your body" and "Come back to your body."

I was starting to grow into the idea that I should better care for this place I lived within. So, we became acquaintances, my body and me.

And then this body of mine, this entity I was making friends with, went and got herself pregnant. In that moment, when the plus sign appeared on the EPT stick, it was like I slowly dropped from above my body down into her. I came home for the first time since childhood.

The divide between being just outside of me and existing within myself dissolved, and I took up residence at my own personal address.

The divide between being just outside of me and existing within myself dissolved, and I took up residence at my own personal address. However, I moved in only as a renter, not quite yet an owner. And I had a roommate—the little love inside of me.

I was growing this baby, and she was growing me. It was just us. No one else could do the job of caring for her but me. I had to take great care of myself, too, for her to have what she needed. I loved every second of my pregnancy. Oh sure, I was irritated that I couldn't tie my shoes after a certain point, and it didn't feel great when her foot seemed to latch onto my bottom rib. But mostly, I felt like a magnificent walking miracle. I was one of those obnoxious glowing mamas-to-be, and I make no apologies for it. It was a gift I needed for both of us. As my baby girl was growing in size, I was growing in power. And wonder. And self.

Having just moved into myself, I wanted to know the full capacity of my strength. I planned a natural birth from day one. I read books, talked with other natural birthing moms, and even watched videos that looked like 70s birth porn of moms giving birth in baby pools in their living rooms and on Ina May Gaskins' farm. I trained like someone who had never put on running shoes but had been signed up for a marathon.

I was my baby's cocoon, and she was my metamorphosis.

When the day came for her to come earthside, I was ready. My body was made for and meant for this moment, to bring forth this babe through birth. I wanted to feel all of it. To be in all of it. My mind was set on the single focus of getting her here. I swept fear to the side and invited the experience in confidence. My spirit was strong and bursting at the seams with worship as my natural delivery felt supernatural. My body contracted and contorted until it unfurled and ushered her into the atmosphere this side of heaven. I experienced the full expression of one of the things my body was made for.

And she was born. And so too was part of me.

She emerged from me, and I emerged into the knowing of my own power.

It would still take more time for me to learn how to inhabit my physical self in full, to embrace my body as its owner. But experiencing my daughter's birth, to see her come into this world in physical form, birthed from my own, it accelerated the path. The sense of profound respect and empowerment of what our bodies can do, what mine could do, made my soul settle in all the more.

A LETTER REGARDING UNREALISTIC EXPECTATIONS

"Yours is the light by which my spirit's born:
You are my sun, my moon, and all my stars."
— E.E. Cummings[3]

Dear Ben,

It's 2002. I am driving down I-75 southbound listening to a CD that you made me with the volume cranked. The sun is shining on this beautiful morning that will hit seventy-four degrees for the high. There is no traffic, so I am moving with ease as the odometer reads just above the speed limit. I realize I am smiling alone in my car. Images of my old life get farther away in the rearview mirror as I fantasize about our future together.

You will be an exceptional husband. You will adore me and always speak softly and with patience to me. You will lead our future family in our faith and in our home. We will make adorable babies, and I will stay at home with these little clones of you. I may even homeschool them. We will have dinner around our table set with care most every night. You will fill my heart and my life with love, affirming the deepest parts of my soul as worthy and loveable. We will have a near-perfect everything.

I am counting the minutes until I see you again. Each of us could close our eyes and find our way to the other's front door. We were made to make the drive. We were made for a life together. We were made for each other.

B, you and I were rattled by disappointment when things didn't unfold like our dreams. Our emotions surrounding the corners of real-life against the soft contours of our idealistic vision ranged from frustration to anger to malaise and back again.

Looking back, the scariest part is that we truly thought we'd live this idyllic life straight out of the movies. We really did think we were putting our true selves forward, but I suppose we may have just been getting to know ourselves . . . ourselves.

When there has been the wanting for something, and you've subconsciously invested time in building up your expectation around it, and then it really happens, well, there's a crash with reality about what really is.

How foolish of us to project such unrealistic expectations onto each other, onto our relationship.

And when you are counting on someone to be your god (or your sun, your moon, and all your stars, as E.E. Cummings writes), and and they fall off their throne (or out of the sky), it's easy to understand how your world can fall apart. It was so easy to allow myself to be pulled into your orbit with your incredible talent and your zest for life.

And so, in order to keep your devotion, I began to whittle myself into the shape of the idol I thought you needed.

Instead of saying, "Well, this is the me you get," I said, "Well, maybe I can become what you need." I kept trying to glue the image you had of me back together instead of gluing *myself* back together.

I began to try to shape you into what I thought you were supposed to be. You started fading away from me when I wasn't who you imagined I would be. You didn't look adoringly or speak kindly or have patience. And neither did I.

And we nearly lost our marriage.
And we nearly lost each other.
And we nearly lost ourselves.

We didn't really try to find our way back, back to the original idealistic vision, back to the romantic playlists and the sentimentalized notions of family life.

Instead, we showed all our cards and dug up our secrets and took off our masks.

We drew all our demons out into the arena, and we began to slay each one of them. We were exhausted. Too exhausted to be anything except just what we were. Too tired to expect perfection. And then we had to decide if the mess we made of things was enough to fight for.

As it turns out, it actually was.
Because it was finally right. And raw. And real.

I'm so sorry I ever laid that mantle on your shoulders, the one you were never meant to bear. And I'm so sad you ever put a yoke on me that I tried so hard to carry. And I'm sorry for the unrealistic expectations we had of each other that we never could live up to. I'm sorry that I let the truth of who we could be together be eclipsed by some sort of make-believe or infatuation.

When you've dreamed about being with someone for so long, and you finally get to, you imagine it's going to be a fairytale, even though life has already shown you that those aren't real. It wasn't your job to rescue me from my princess tower, with its fables of saccharine happy endings, because I needed to learn how to rescue myself. Ours has been a love story with a few chapters I wish were never written and others that exceed what I ever could have dreamed. You have been the reason I've sharpened my sword of self-protection and the one who slowly dismantled my armor with love. The scope of the story stretches way above the highs and lows and tears and repairs, and the songs in our hearts are still singing each other's names.

One of the most beautiful freedoms for me came the moment I heard a voice inside of me say, "If you can detach from him, then you can really connect with him." That was such a turning point for me.

There's no non-stop flight from those early years to the goodness of Now. Likewise, we aren't guaranteed there won't be turbulence from here, and it's a safe bet that there will be. But I'm so glad that we've stayed the course. Isn't it a beautiful journey, really, this life we're creating and recreating? You/I/We have been worth this fight.

You are now not, in fact, my sun, my moon, or all of my stars, and that's probably one of the most loving things I could say to you. I have come out from the shadows of delusion and have learned to shine my brightest *beside* you instead of behind or beneath you.

I asked you the other day what you loved most about the Now Us. Without hesitation, you offered, "You're not trying to be what you think I want. I'm not trying to be something I think you want. We're just us, together."

I love that. And you. We are lifers.

Love,
Me

TREND

I'm sitting in my favorite local coffee shop. In walks a tall woman with short thick bouncy hair and a sincere smile who announces with her quilted embroidered bag that she is "Blessed." A few seats down from me, I see a table of women gathered doing a Bible study. I'm not sure if there is a leader but, if I had to choose one, it would be the lady with the t-shirt that reads, "Called." Tattoos of testimony are also sprinkled throughout the cafe, and there are stickers on surrounding Hydro Flasks: Faith over Fear, Be Strong and Courageous, and Y'all Need Jesus.

I can't help but wonder . . .

Are these signs of Christ or the emblems of membership? If not, "They will know we are Christians by our love," then will we tell them with our apparel?

Either way, I felt on the outside. And acutely aware that so much of the social context of my zip code is this sort of fad, the Southeast Regional Conference of Kingdom Fashion.

I sat on the edge of this suddenly obvious trend and felt how I typically do in conservative religious circles: Out of place.

If I had a t-shirt announcing my insides in a one-liner, it might be: "One of these ducks is not like the other."

Please understand, I tell you in earnest that I am not trying to be critical toward these folks or their outfits. The truth is that even though it's a little off-putting for me now, I do recall a time when that style checked out for me.

I used to bear the stripes of their tribe. And I missed being a part of it that day in the coffee shop.

Having known the feeling of fitting in with them and then choosing to leave has maybe been more isolating than having never been a part of it in the first place.

Anyway, I don't.

Belong.

With them.

And a great sadness swept over me.

Sad that Sunday mornings didn't make sense to me the way they used to.

Sad that I was not a part of that sweet community any longer.

And I felt suffocated by that sadness for a long moment.

I ordered a tea to go and headed to the park. I sat at the base of a tree and let Creation whisper with its wind, "You belong to Me." It was like my face had been lightly stroked by the hand of God, much the way I tenderly brush my hand on the faces of my girls when I'm assuring them of my love or the promise that things are going to be alright.

The sadness didn't leave. But gratefulness swept over me and joined it.

It's another of those both/and moments I find myself living in quite a bit these days . . .

Grateful for meeting God so beautifully outside of the brick and mortar.

Grateful for the deconstruction and the rebuilding.

Grateful for the Beautiful Mystery.

In the interest of truth-telling and embracing irony, you have to know that my daughter came back from camp a week after my coffee shop experience with a shirt that reads, "I exist to proclaim the gospel." Jesus.

I mean, I take responsibility. I am the one who had "Camp Pickup" marked on Saturday in my calendar and knew she would be at camp for four days but told her to pack enough shirts for three. My solution once we realized there was a day we hadn't accounted for? Here's a twenty—grab a t-shirt at the camp store. And that t-shirt is what she chose. I mean, I'm sure there were plenty of options, but that's the one she got. The irony of this does not evade me.

Maybe we can't help ourselves. We want to belong; we want others to be able to spot us out in the wilds of life and see that we are kinsmen. Maybe we're afraid of feeling lonely. Maybe our matching merchandising is our medicine for that loneliness.

But maybe, just maybe, God needs to get us alone to get us to listen. To the Voice that matters above all the one-note choir of belonging around us.

Maybe we need to feel lonely once in a while until we understand our deepest longing to be a part of something can only find resolution with the Divine.

And perhaps the way to proclaim the gospel is to live it out. Not to wear it out.

ANXIETY

There's a competition that goes on in my head like a battle of the bands. It's the voice of reason versus the voice of anxiety, and I'm telling you, there are times it feels like it's a deathmatch. Take, for example, the following examples of internal yelling matches:

Reason: R / Anxiety: A

R: I turned off the curling iron.

A: I'm not sure I turned off the curling iron. In fact, I probably didn't. I'm sure I didn't. I'm going to burn the house down.

R: I'm so sad she had a bad day at school, but I know these are learning and growing opportunities.

A: She's isolated and lonely, and she's going to make terrible life choices as a result of this one moment because you know everything that happens to us is just a string of dots connecting on our life path, and she is going to operate out of a deep well of sadness forever because of this one moment.

R: I made a mistake.

A: I make mistakes all the time because I am a mistake maker, and I can't get my shit together. Dumb. Dumb.

Dumb. Dumb. Dumb. (And then a string of mistakes follows because I am anxious about making mistakes that I can't think clearly enough to find my way outside of making them.)

R: Social event = This might be fun! I'll get to catch up with so many people!

A: Social event = Death by chit-chat. Maybe I can come late and leave early. And ugh! I hope I'm not too awkward.

R: Time for bed. I'm ready to rest, and I can easily fall asleep.

A: I'm exhausted. But I can't sleep. I need to set my alarm. Eyes close, begin to settle, re-check the alarm because even though I physically remember setting it three times within the last eight minutes, I am sure it will not be going off in the morning because I have failed to do it correctly or there is a glitch or whatever—I bet it's not set.

R: (Morning alarm sounds) It's the start of a new day. Fresh hope!

A: (Morning alarm sounds—if you're not already awakened by the fear that your alarm won't go off . . . Or insert any other fear here). "It's here. Okay. I feel calm. Nope. I was just too sleepy to register how tight my chest is. Still, I can do this. I think. I mean, I can. I have to. Here I go."

R: That email I sent to my client was clear and concise.

A: What if my client thinks I'm being short or hurried? Should I send a follow-up email? Wait, that'll make me look like I WAS being short and realized it, and that would suggest something they may not be thinking to begin with? But they could be thinking it. Gosh, they probably are thinking it. IDIOT!

At times the voice of Anxiety has been so urgent and hyperventilating and that it sounds like the absolute Truth. It is nearly impossible to unravel myself from its grip in those moments.

Other times the voice is in my native tongue of sarcasm, and the tone of her messages are exasperated at the drama of it all. I imagine her rolling her eyes.

As I've learned to manage my anxiety (because I've had so much opportunity to practice), I can *sometimes* extract myself from it just long enough to see its ugly face and recognize it for what it is. I can whisper to my spirit that this is temporary. As the emotional bombs go off in my mind, I know that things are being filtered through the lens of Anxiety instead of Reason, and so, even though I can't necessarily get my bearings altogether, I can remind myself not to latch onto the present internal chaos.

When I woke up to my life in sobriety, a lot of things were bright and beautiful. But there was still a lot of unconquered territory. For me, I drank to quiet the demons. And all of them were waiting for me when the bottle ran dry. Anxiety was one of them. When it came over me like a tidal wave, and I didn't have Tito's to numb it, I felt like I had hives on the inside that I couldn't scratch. Anxiety is pesky and persistent, usually unpredictable and always inconvenient, and ranges from nagging to taunting.

Sometimes I can point to all of the things and assuredly say, "Yep. It makes complete sense that I'd be anxious right now." Maybe I didn't sleep but a few hours and it's been a day of disciplining with the girls and I ate sugary crap that whacked out my mood and Ben and I got irritated with each other and I'm in boiler room-like counter offers on two different deals with timelines that overlap and I've got to sing a song with high notes that are a stretch for me and I'm overscheduled all the way around. Good chance I'm set up for the Anxiety Body Snatcher to move on in and mess with me. I've set the stage for her.

Other times life is rolling along smoothly, and then BAM! That MFer of Anxiety blindsides me and hijacks my joy. Just like that. No warning at all. The uninvited guest shows up unannounced to crash the party of my good day. It sticks a tube into my chest, drains out all of my peace, and pumps unreasonable fear into my soul.

No matter how or when it attacks me, there are a few things I try to do to bring me back to baseline:

— Trace each finger.

— Practice yoga.

— Count my steps.

— Go for a run.

— Do breathing exercises.

— Listen to the quiet.

— Take a bath.

Those things bring me back to my body, and I am reminded that the Divine lives inside, and so the peace and love that I need is right inside of me if I can just get myself to access it.

To his credit, Ben is incredible in these moments. Like healing balm. Day or night (or middle of the night when I wake him). He locks eyes with me and doesn't get annoyed if I reroute my gaze because I can't focus. He just draws me back to him. He puts his hand on my pounding chest and breathes with me. When my breathing slows, he asks, "What do we need to do right now for you?" (And then he helps me take steps to do that.)

He reminds me of who I am, what is true, and what is false about the narrative my mind is spinning. He also never lets me forget that there is another side where I don't feel like this, and I'll be there soon. And sometimes "soon" is a couple of hours, and sometimes the tourniquet of Anxiety tightens its grip around me for days. Days of physical angst, mental boxing matches, and emotional exhaustion.

Eventually, it does begin to let up. And over time, the inner pendulum finds more manageable sways until it's oscillating at regular rhythms. The Anxiety has passed, and I am safe again as my pulse begins to beat proportionately to and in Reality.

SHAME

I've already disclosed to you my love of mopping and my bone-deep need for a tidy house.

I wish life could clean up as easily as my kitchen.

That we could look at the splats and gunk in our hearts and just wipe them away with a bit of elbow grease and vinegar in minutes.

But that's not how it works.

Rerouting reactions, retraining the tongue, and learning to listen better—those kinds of things take serious time.

If I'm triggered to respond to something in an old way and give in to emotional presets or insistent interruptions, I can fall apart on the inside. I bury myself under the rubble of shame that I have run through the Shit Cycle again.

I think part of my confusion in reconciling shame was how I understood the idea of laying things at the feet of Jesus. I thought that it was like mopping.

Did you ever go to church camp or a retreat where you wrote your sins down on a piece of paper? (Sidebar: I always found that scrap of paper exceptionally small for my personal sin list.) You nailed it to a cross, reminding you that Jesus took on your sins. Another spin on that camp activity was putting a letter of confession in a paper bag and then pitching it in a bonfire to illustrate your sins burning away.

My young mind thought I'd get up from that auditorium chair or circle of campers suddenly sin-free, the only evidence being the ash cross put on my cheek from the cooled sin-fire. So, you can imagine the disappointment when I tripped over the same snares so quickly after "sanctification."

When I faced off with sin, and it won, shame slithered over me and pressed down on me like an astronaut experiencing full gravity after returning to Earth. Think two hundred eighty pounds of emotional immobility. How could I have picked all my junk back up and put it back inside of my heart so quickly? S h a m e on me.

The catalog of trespasses to avoid seemed to shift according to my faith community, so the list of "thou shalt nots" was exhaustive. It spanned the likes of rated R movies, v-neck t-shirts, secular music, "bad" words, wine. Also on the naughty list was gossiping (which is not the same as adding someone's "situation" to the group prayer list, ahem . . .), eating according to the Maker's design, and taming that tingly feeling between my legs that I'd get when the cute quarterback walked in the room.

Also, these rights and wrongs were black and white. Being someone who has historically sucked at moderation, I at first found comfort in the categories of absolutes. But over time, as some of the things on the naughty list would vary and shift, I wondered if there might be other perspectives to consider the same "wrongdoings." Could there be gray? Even amendments? Was there possibly something more important to consider, like intent and motive and heart? Could there be a whole new way of looking at something altogether?

All important questions, because living with a continual low hum of shame, no matter what you're doing or not doing or trying not to do, can undoubtedly drown out any victory song in your life.

But the opposite of shame is not calling olly olly oxen free on every behavior in the book and calling it all subjective anyway. We can't just pitch the entire idea of moving ourselves away from things that are bad for us—bad for our souls, bad for our bodies, bad for our hearts—as somehow trying to avoid shame.

A counselor told me many years ago that the "thing" (whatever it is) that you don't want to do can become the thing you're trying not to do, and then eventually, that thing can become something you only do sometimes. And ultimately, with hope and practice, it can become the thing you used to do.

A while back, I read Richard Rohr's perspective of repentance. He said, "'Repent' . . . quite literally means 'to change your mind.'"[4] That undertaking seems like it takes time. Like it's an invitation to eventually grow in a different way. It means that I can both see the danger certain behaviors have put me in and I can decide to do better, without carrying the burden of shame with me.

Those bits of wisdom began to lift the weight of the shame suit and cycle for me. I can intentionally grow into something else. I can change my mind about things to where I begin to operate out of that new knowledge instead of my old way of thinking. Surely I can do that. And how beautiful a process that could be.

I love the popular quote that someone probably first wittily said at a girls' night but that has now turned into t-shirts on Amazon: "If cauliflower can somehow become pizza . . . you, my friend, can do anything."

If we just stick with the process, we can get to the other side of things. We can evolve into a new and better mindset. Equally important perhaps, we can get to the other side of shame. (And if nothing else, we can bury our troubles in pizza with any crust of our choosing.)

> **If we just stick with the process, we can get to the other side of things. We can evolve into a new and better mindset. Equally important perhaps, we can get to the other side of shame.**

DIRTY LITTLE SECRET

I have a dirty little secret.
I'm not proud of it.

I feel nervous and sick to write it.

Also embarrassed.

But here it is.

I get jealous.

Specifically, I can get jealous of my friends.

I don't mean jealous like, "Oh wow! You get a date night out at that awesome restaurant? Jelly!!"

I mean J e a l o u s.

Ugh. Gross. Blah.

It is the thing I wish more than anything was different about me.

It is distracting.

If left unchecked, it can be relentless.

To.be.clear: I'm not jealous over t h i n g s.

I love your new car, and I don't want it. You look fabulous in that sweater, and I hope you bought one in every color for yourself! Your new home addition is exquisite! I'm so happy for you! You got the promotion! Do the damn thing! I'm completely stoked for you!

I don't want your material things or successes at all.

No.

That's not it.

It's that I can get jealous of r e l a t i o n s h i p s.

It can go like this.

My left hand is holding my phone as my right index finger scrolls the Instagram images on the screen and the portrayal of perfect moments are on display for me (and the world) to see.

Even though I know the curator has taken the time to perfect her post and choose the most flattering filter, some things can still bruise my heart.

Like the vacation some friends took together with other families we don't hang out with.
Their caption: Best. Vacay. Ever.
(Sounds like it topped the one we took with them.)

Or the close friends who went to dinner without me but with others.
(Is that their new crew?)

Or the party we didn't get an invite to.
(Wonder why we didn't make the cut?)

Or I walk into a cafe and see a circle of friends having lunch.
Or ice cream together with their kids after the first day of school.
Or I hear about their weekend campout in conversation at the pool.

Isn't that ridiculous? Like, I'm g r o w n. A grown UP. Closer to fifty than I am to forty.

But when the inner dialogue begins, it's not even my current voice. I hear the hurt in the voice of a younger me. I call her "Middle School Mel."
She's not petty or dramatic.
She just wants to be included.
She's on the fringe of your circle and just wants to be invited in.

To be wanted.

Sometimes when I see pics and posts or hear weekend recaps, my heart goes back to that front stoop, and someone is picking the other friend over me. And I'm eclipsed by the emotion of not being good enough/cool enough/like them enough to be asked to come along.

And the truth is, I don't so much want to come along all the time as I want to be asked to join. I just want what I perceive that they have: a true sense of Belonging. Even more, I'd love for them to feel like my being part of their group would add to their sense of belonging. That they'd want to belong with me.

I have some incredible friends, to be sure. But some of the women I'm closest with one-on-one might not easily mesh. My collection of confidants is loving and present. I do have belonging. I just don't belong to very many. And they don't all belong to each other.

As life ebbs and flows and friends move or kids change schools or are in different activities or a person starts a job or quits work to stay home or whatever and anything, there can be shifts in friendships. It's a normal, natural thing about life. But it's never made those transitions easier for me. It's tough for me to see a new tribe form because of different circumstances. Especially when I thought I had a home with those friends. And it's not about falling out or "breaking up" with them. I see them out and it's warm and huggy and gosh, when can we catch up? But in certain seasons there's just no window for connection. They are sitting in bleachers next to other moms cheering on kids and I'm at a field or in an audience with mine next to different families. They see each other every Sunday at church while our family is having brunch. They all got redistricted to the same school and we are starting over at another school even though we live one street over from them. These things all add up, but they are just hard for me. I can get worked up in my head writing stories about close-knit groups and all they're enjoying together and bonding over.

When I run out of mental material, social media feeds the narrative. And I sort of wilt inside.

I have found that I bruise most easily when I am tired or overrun with work. For a number of years, I was frazzled from uprooting our family every weekend when we lived in our Airbnb and we would have to remove ourselves from our home premises for guests. If my to-do list is maxed out and there's no space for creativity or quiet, I'm not at my best. And when my life is unbalanced, it is harder to navigate everything. So, in those moments when I pass a group of friends taking a walk together or scroll through posts of dinner and drinks, it stings way more than when I'm rested or fulfilled in my own life. When I've had sweet time with my girls and Ben or when I've had a rich conversation with a friend on my back porch or when I've got writing flowing or music brewing, those waters are way easier to wade. Because then I feel a deep sense of belonging to my family, to my friends, and to my art. And I'm not so hungry for what's on another's plate or Instagram page.

I'll tell you an interesting thing. Writing this out has lifted some of its weight. It's the keeping of the secret that gives it power. You've given me a confessional closet here, reading my struggle with this particular emotion. Putting it out there didn't eradicate it. But just processing through it in words has reminded me that it is just a *thing*. It's a feeling, a strong one, but it is not me. It is something I wrestle with and that I can, over time, hopefully, pin down for the count.

IMPRINTS

Annie's tearful eyes were fixed on mine and were full of fear. The nurse promised to be quick and gentle, but my shaky six-year-old had already seen all the empty vials they were planning to fill with her blood samples. She had been experiencing unexplained stomach pain, and the doctor was ruling out an array of food allergies. While at it, she was also assessing blood counts for assurance that there was no chance of a Wilms tumor like the one that took my brother. The quick process seemed to last an hour. I put my forehead up against Annie's, and we breathed in together—inhale peace . . . exhale fear. Her usual easy-go-lucky demeanor was now terrified. She sat as still as she could during the draw, but as soon as it was over, she came all the way unglued. She cried uncontrollably and begged for us to promise her she'd never have to do that again. She was gasping for sips of air like one does during a hard cry, and I held her body, hot from panic, in my arms until she was able to slow her breathing. Ben drove while I sat in the back seat with her. She put her head on my chest and held tight to both of my hands. She had a hard time coming back into herself that night, in a daze from the experience.

Five years later, Annie still comes undone when someone simply extends their arm, inner elbow exposed. If it's one of us three Hardins, she'll beg, "Please! You know I don't like that!" If it's anyone else, she'll slide out of the circle and take refuge where she can't see it.

When she has a doctor's appointment, she'll ask right out of the gate if she has to get a needle again. It would be easy to tell her to pull it together and that she was being exaggerative, but I could see her response was sincere. For her, the whole thing was traumatizing.

It's a thing. A real thing. Her initial experience continues to inform her current circumstances.

I get it, Annie. Oh, how I understand, baby.

Cancer.

I blinked my eyes into focus and scrolled back to the top of the text box. Surely I read that wrong. I studied each word again and read the sentence in a whispered voice to make sure I understood this right.

Yes, that is what it read: Cancer.

My dear friend and sister of my heart, Katye texted that the lump she found in her breast weeks ago was, in fact, cancer.

The prognosis was promising, all things considered. And her peace with the matter was evident, as steady assurance in her Healer is her signature. She noted that she knew that I would pray for her and ended her message with, "I can't tell you how faithful and close God is. Truly, closer than my breath."

But I couldn't even catch my breath.

I fell all the way apart.

Into the pit of past grief that sucked me down into its despair before I could even put my phone on the counter.

Even though we were just one step down the road of Katye's, I could not help but consider the painstaking path traveled with another friend.

Hers was a six-year journey through cancer. And it was relentless and ruthless.

Even though I prayed.

There were text strings back then with updates: "Prayer warriors, good job! Surgery went well. God is good!"

And others: "Prayer warriors, keep it up. Not out of the woods. Keep believing and trusting!"

We all prayed.

We stormed the gates of heaven with fervent intercession.

We claimed the gates of hell would not prevail.

We sang praise and worship over her broken body and called it whole.

And then she died.

She died anyway, even though we begged for it to turn out another way.

So, if God is good because the surgery went well, then does that mean the converse, that God is not good when my friend died? I don't think so. But it seems like a safer play for my heart to just let God do what God wants to do and not work so hard to move the needle.

Back to a few days ago, when that new message from Katye came across my phone.

I panicked when I read the diagnosis. And again when I read the trust she had in me to pray. It's not that I didn't want to pray. It's that I didn't know how to anymore. Not about this, for sure.

Even if I could get over the hurdle of confusion from my most recent experience, there was still this other voice from the past competing for my peace. The one that felt compelled to tell my parents that their little boy died because of their lack of faith.

The fact pattern taught me that I better pray good and hard and just right, or it's not going down like I'm asking for it to.

So now what?

Grief eclipsed my ability to respond to my friend with strength.

I was swallowed up by fear.

In my anguish, I cried out. But not to God. I wasn't ready to talk to God just yet. Any other time, I may have reached out to Katye when I got news like this. Along the course of our friendship, it's me leaning on the strength of her faith. Not the other way around.

I reached for the lifeline of my friend Lisa, she of the pride confession I had made about having my kids clean the kitchen. I needed the balm of her words to help me make sense of things. Truth be told, I was begging her. To tell me how to pray. To pray for me.

What should I say?

How should I say it?

I just don't know the words, you know?

How do you pray when the prescribed prayers of your past now have a black box warning?

I just don't know if I can do it.

The cloud of terror was like a thick, murky mass that loomed overhead, and I let it envelop me. I couldn't see anything but the storm.

Lisa helped me boil things down to a simple form of Yes and No. Instead of long-winded pronouncements or bold demands, I aligned my thoughts (and eventually my prayers) with Yes and No.

I could not form these words at first. Just deep cries and groans that bore witness to my weakness. But God met me there even when I didn't want to pray. Even when I was angry. Especially when I was weak. God is not just in the light. God is there, too, in the shadows.

God is not just in the light. God is there, too, in the shadows.

It took me hours to respond to Katye's diagnosis message. I had to find a clearing in the clouds so that she was not left to manage my reaction. I was going to be there for her, and it was not time for me to be needy or wavering.

Yes to her continued peace.
Yes to healing energy to flow through her.
Yes to clear scans.
Yes to her being closely held.
Yes to something surprisingly beautiful in the midst of this.

No to fear.
No to resilient harmful cells.
No to growth of the wrong things.

Yes to trusting that God will hold her. And me.
No to being sure of much of anything but that.

I'm still a long way from knowing how to deal with the emotions of fear and uncertainty and grief that envelop my heart. But I know too there's something, something inside of me still reaching out to God when dark is all I can see. I don't know what He'll do in this circumstance. I don't understand how it all works. But I'm saying yes to peace in the pitch-black.

Eclipsed by the Past

The specter of your childhood, your history, that unfortunate choice you made in high school, those voices that shaped your days, it all can shade your today. It can sometimes be hard to recognize when you are living in a shadow of a past experience; after all—our memories, our joys, our hurts, they all help sculpt who we are. But sometimes, the hard edge of an event marks the line between you and living a life fully in the light.

ABOUT BRENT

Dinner at our house was strained. Dad was usually at some board meeting or on the golf course, and he'd scoot in just in time for us all to sit down. Mom was toggling between reheating one of her rotating chicken dishes and refilling her signature tall yellow plastic cup with vodka and Diet Pepsi. If my older brother Lewis was there, his eyes were usually hazy, and, clear or not, his gaze trailed off to where he'd rather be: anywhere but here. Sadness stretched out to the corners of the ceiling like a visceral veil and hung heaviest above the round oak table where we sat trying our best to be normal at a table set for four instead of five. The grief from the loss of my brother Brent was ever-present, even this many years later. At family dinner, it was as palpable to our palates as the too-seasoned potatoes Mom had roasted. An ever-present lump in our throats.

Brent died when he was just six years old. Cancer ripped him from my parents' praying hands. My older brother Lewis was eight when his world collided with tragedy. I was just around seven months old. The trajectory of my family's fate forever changed when he left the earth. I can't explain exactly how it was for everyone else. Looking in from the outside, you might generally say that Lewis struggled to escape grief and acted out as a result, and that my parents' marriage reflected their mourning. My mom says that Lewis just sort of disappeared when Brent died . . . and then kept on disappearing for a long time. About her marriage, she divulged that she and my father dealt with their grief differently, found themselves in emotional chaos, and each had their ways of numbing their sorrow for a great while.

And then there was me. The only one I can really tell you about. (The only one any of us can really tell the truth about.)

For me, growing up in the shadow of Brent's life and death was complicated.

It was kind of like nursing a wound my whole family had without anyone asking me to and without really understanding what they needed. It was complicated by the fact that, given that I was still a baby when he died, I didn't really know him. But I certainly knew his ghost.

It was like living out a narrative with one would-be lead character smudged out of the storyline. Like sitting around that dinner table staring at the empty chair that Brent should be in but would never sit in again.

I always felt like I was looking into whatever situation or moment we were in as a family and re-imagining what it would be like if a fifth member were to be a part of it. Would the three faces that I was looking at have a lighter countenance? Would there be greater joy in the air? Would they be getting along better? Would there just be more ease overall?

But I couldn't get lost in those considerations. After all, I was busy.

Busy building a dam to blunt the erosion of my family's happiness. Busy trying to buffer the tension of the teenage years between my parents and brother. Busy being chatty to smooth out the contrived conversation between them. Busy being adorable so as to brighten the darkness. Busy trying to glue everyone back together with my beaming little girl eyes and wide little girl smile and sweet little girl love.

Everyone else also felt Brent's absence but didn't dare speak of it. It felt like they all expected more of one another to fill the void of the one who wasn't there. And that is taxing, as you can imagine. Taking on the role of the proverbial hero child, I launched into life ready and willing to please and never feeling like I was enough. Not because no one praised me. But it's exceptionally exhausting when you're trying to do the work of just being yourself and then also trying to be the superhero sibling of the mourning brother and the easy, wonderful, disciplined, smart, perfect child for the mourning parents. It was constant emotion-managing acrobatics.

I worshipped at the altar of my older brother, and I chased every carrot unintentionally dangled in front of my face by my parents to please away their pain.

By the time I got into high school, I didn't really know who I was outside of jumping through everyone's hoops of perceived needs. But I still didn't know much about whose shoes I was trying to fill. I may have asked a few questions over those years, but mostly I collected clues about my freckle-faced strawberry blond brother from comments peppered throughout my childhood.

Brent was a mystery in the most beautiful, wonderful, magnetic way. I was drawn to his memory though I only heard fragments of it. Sometimes I thought everyone around me was trying to outrun his memory, but I realized later that they were just trying to keep one step in front of their relentless grief. And they would memorialize him when and how they could.

When I look back at the fractured and sometimes fragile family from that time, I want to encourage them with what's a ways down the road but coming nonetheless. Restoration. Redemption. Relationship. I want to show them how they all manage to regain joy in their respective ways. And I'd love to tell Little Girl Me that they all get there without much help from her. That way, she can just breathe and be and enjoy her dinner.

FRONT STOOP

We are outside on the front stoop of my house at 924 Miller Avenue after half-day kindergarten. I'm with the girl I consider my best friend. I'll call her Molly. My mom is in charge of looking after us on this particular afternoon while Molly's mother works at the sewing shop on Washington Street. Molly's family moved to town and diagonally behind us in Bayne Acres Subdivision when I was two. Coincidentally, Molly and I were the same age and even shared a birthday. I remember thinking that we were magically connected like sisters, likely because I longed for one, and this was the next best thing. We played together regularly, and though I can recall bits of those moments with vagueness, this afternoon in 1981 is seared into my memory with absolute clarity.

Something is troubling me. I have a question for Molly, and I'm hesitant, even afraid to hear her answer. But I have to know it.

My eyes are panning from the grass just in front of me to the trunk of the oak tree at the side of my yard. The concrete steps feel warm beneath me, and the overcast sky offers a mild breeze in our direction. My thin chestnut brown hair sweeps over my face with the wind, and I brush it back out of my eyes to reveal a face of fragility. Molly sits to my right in her much cuter outfit, carefree as I struggle beside her. Having recently started at Southside Elementary, we have met many new friends at school. I suppose I have noticed Molly taking attention away from me to focus on other friends, especially a dainty girly girl blonde I'll call Sarah. My cotton t-shirts and skinned-up knees look out of place next to their perfect French braids and pressed preppy clothes and Stride Rite shoes.

Have I lost my rank?

Finally, "So . . . Is Sarah your new best friend now, or am I still it?"

Molly immediately wiggles uncomfortably and diverts her eyes away from me.

I know.

But still, I wait for her to announce the verdict.

She utters, "Well . . . I don't wanna hurt your feelings, but . . . It's Sarah."

I sink. Tears race to their ducts. Sheer will keeps them from falling. I correct my slump with projected proud posture and counter with something upbeat and understanding, "Oh, it's OK. I get it. It's fine! Really!" I pop off the porch to distract from any evidence of heartbreak.

Then the whole memory ends like a light fading away in a scene of a movie I wish I never saw.

That was my very first memory.

My first sting of rejection.

My first runner-up ribbon.

My first, "There's someone else."

But not my last.

I got the message early on: "You are not enough." And what's more, "Someone else is." When I look back on that day, I wish I hadn't asked at all. Or that Molly naming Sarah as her new best friend didn't burrow into my heart and take up so much space. I mean, my God, I'm sure she never could've imagined the ripple effect of that conversation. Truly, neither could I. I've spent years trying to unhear those words. But life has had a way of reiterating them.

I can see now that this grade school rejection stayed planted for years to come, a nightshade species which finds its fullest flower when stress and hurt and a bitter word from someone take a moon-lit dance around my heart. I don't want to think something so typical, something so predictable as being the kindergarten best friend reject, could still cast such a long shadow. But that's the nature of shadow, after all; it's bigger than the reality of what it reflects.

> **That's the nature of shadow, after all; it's bigger than the reality of what it reflects.**

As a kid, things can feel bigger than they actually are. Like the spot where we used to play king of the hill. My memory recounts that the neighbors and I would ascend to the top of the steep incline of our side yard and playfully push the king from his position to the plight of his downslope. Now I shake my head at that recollection. The "steep incline" is hardly that at all. In fact, it's barely a mound. Maybe we feel and see things so big as kids because all the world around us eclipses us in size. I'm not sure. Either way, our perceptions can create topography for our expectations to come. Maybe that's what happened with Molly. She didn't even say what she did to me out of a mean spirit or spite. I pushed her into the truth corner, and she answered with the integrity I asked for.

But still. Even at their best-intentioned, words and rejection and truth, well, they can take root.

Early experiences in rejection burrow deep, and we tuck them down beneath the layers we acquired in our hike through life. The calluses of blistering experiences in early days, particularly those childhood days, guard patches where we used to be pliable, where we used to be soft.

But given enough time, given enough sheets of hardened skin to mask the pain, the calluses of the past affect how we hike today. We adjust our stride, walk differently to bypass those scarred spots. Which means we rub new blisters into fresh flesh, all in an attempt to avoid what caused the original welts.

DUMPSTER

All my secrets were kept safe inside of it. My Grandmom Maddox had given it to me as a birthday gift. Like her, it was fancy. The hardback cover was crimson, and "My Diary" was in gold lettering to match the trim of the pages. There was a lock to keep watch over my words. There wasn't much to dish in the fourth grade, but that didn't stop me from filling its lined pages. It held a range of classified information, from details about my grade-school crushes to my eagerness for my buds to become full-grown boobs. I distinctly remember an entry about how my heart broke when my uncle died unexpectedly in a car accident. I learned that by putting my hurts into words, it helped my heart heal. And so along I went, keeping journals throughout middle school and high school and into college. The scoop got juicier as I kept records of milestones like rounding the proverbial bases with a boy and moving away from my hometown. I would also pen prayers and wonder in words about all my big God questions.

The collection of these pages chronicled my personal history from age nine to nineteen. They were priceless to me, and I even carted the heavy box of them off to college and continued to add to it through my sophomore year at the University of Kentucky.

And then along came a boy. A boy I wanted to love me. A boy I thought might just love me. A boy who found one of my journals one night. And read it. And in it, I had questioned our relationship. I had also written about a moment in my past that didn't include him. Something that came up in a dream. A subconscious recollection of an earlier time in my life, innocent really. But it was enough to set him off. He was a grenade with the pin out. That's the most accurate way to describe him. And he was about to blow. He wanted answers. He wanted to know why I would even think about someone else ever again besides him. Was I sneaking around behind his back? Did I have lingering feelings about someone else?

Was I fully committed to him? How could I prove my loyalty to him? Show him how much he meant to me? That the past was really behind me?

I was petrified. Gasping for air and for answers.

It's hard to piece together. I can only see flashes of that night, like lightning. But here's what I do know. Somehow that line of questioning led to us driving to a dumpster behind Lazarus Department Store late at night with that box of journals in the back seat. And the way to prove my fidelity to him was to take those books of memoirs and to throw each one of them in the literal garbage. Because in his mind, I was trash for questioning him, us. And any remnants of my life before him belonged in the actual dumpster. (God help me, this is still so excruciating to remember.)

I don't think I said anything as it was happening, as I was hurling my heart into the ruin. I think I could actually feel it breaking.

I had betrayed myself for him.

And I hated both of us for it. His anger and my own desperation had eclipsed me.

But here's what didn't go into the heap of trash that night. What actually happened in those accounts. I had destroyed the material evidence of the Me before I was his, but that couldn't erase the experiential evidence of that "before" life.

She was still there. Below the surface, for sure. Barely recognizable anymore. But she was in there.

And not being able to visit her through the pages made me mourn for her all the more. Would we ever be together again?

HIM

Once upon a time, I fell for a boy with intoxicating green eyes and mesmerizing charisma who smelled like Abercrombie and Fitch cologne and a whole lotta trouble. Against my better judgment, I let myself be captivated by his charm and wit, and I ignored every intuition that internally screamed: RUN! His veneer was fun-loving, exceedingly affectionate, and absolutely hilarious. But something was always rumbling just below that surface. Like thunder. And I got caught in his storm.

I think I was swept up in the idea that a "bad boy" might change his wandering ways to settle down for me. That would've given me a wealth of worth, to be the girl who one so wild could actually love. There was a hole in my heart that was gaping open, and my self-worth had fallen through it. Then he came along, and I believed that if I could just turn him around, that great feat would only be possible by someone of great worth. Which would mean I would have great worth if I could pull it off.

I think he wanted so badly to be able to settle his turbulent soul, and I looked like a good place to land. Maybe he thought his hot-tempered heart could simmer in my stability. Even now, it's hard to say for sure. We dated off and on for three years, marked by signs that should have proved to us that we were not meant for a life together. Either way that didn't stop us from professing forever in front of a church full of friends and family (and my future husband to boot).

Not surprisingly, our marriage nuptials did not glue our fractured relationship together. In fact, they seemed to mean very little to my new husband. Let's just say they didn't stand in his way of extracurricular activities. Some men collect watches or sports memorabilia. My guy collected women. I'm sure his partners in the periphery got silver-tongued sentiments, but he played dirty when it came to words with me. I got the shrapnel from the exploding bombs of his untended wounds. I believe we all operate from our pain on some level, and his was deep, so the pain he inflicted was deep in turn. The most alarming part was the unpredictability of it all. I'd say if I were to chart the course of his drastic mood swings, they were further apart and less pronounced in the beginning of our marriage, and evolved to shocking shifts and savage soundbites at the end.

I felt so small behind the shadows of his imposing personality. Swallowed up by his daunting presence. I forgot that I used to stand on my own, that I used to shine. Could I again? In the midst of the hopelessness, I'd hear my heart whisper, "There's another life out there you are supposed to be living." I'd never had a hard time speaking up for the underdog. I had a history of it. But I couldn't seem to find that voice on my own behalf. Still, I knew too that if I didn't leave soon, I might disappear altogether.

I held on for as long as I did out of fear. I was terrified of disappointing God if I walked away from him. I knew I had what my church called a "scriptural right" out of our marriage because of his serial infidelity. Still, I would have nightmares about sitting at the Judgment Seat of God and watching Him hold up a divorce decree before He opened up the door to Hell and flung me in there.

One night, in the aftermath of a verbal onslaught and long list of lies, a near-audible voice from heaven swept over me like a wave of permission. I knew I could go. My time had come, and my fight was over. And so, I did. In a calm and sure voice, I told him that I was leaving him and that I was never looking back. I packed my bag, got into my car, and drove away, never even glancing in the rearview mirror.

I still fight the need to mitigate any negative opinions someone might form about me regarding that ill-fated, poison-infused, short-lived, and long-consequence first marriage. The thing is, I just can't weave my words well enough to make everyone understand, and I gave up reputation management some time ago. I think marriage is important. I think vows are important . . . however, I knew it was not only okay but exactly right for me to leave. And that's what I did. I've never doubted that decision. Not for a single second. Oh sure, I grieved, but more for the loss of time and the near-loss of myself. And even for him, for his self-imposed afflictions. But I was not going to be in the wake of his wounds any longer.

I packed up what was left of me, walked out of that darkness, and stepped into a new dawn.

BEN

I think my heart would have always wondered about him if we never got together.

It was his gentle warmth that most drew me to him. I thought he was *like, so cute* back in high school; tall, lean, and sandy-haired with a quiet confidence that held my attention. Still, being over two years older than him, I kept him in the friend zone. That is, until we ran into each other on that perfect fall afternoon behind Patterson Office Tower between classes at the University of Kentucky. He had just transferred there, and I had just broken up with some guy who made me throw my diaries in a dumpster. I can still picture his slow, steady stride across the lawn before we stopped to catch up. My inner voice nudged me; *now? Could this work now?* His heart posed the same question, but we kept our curiosities to ourselves while we built a friendship over late-night conversations after campus ministry groups and mess hall meetups.

We went along this way for several months, neither one of us confessing our mutual crushes. Our looks across the room at one another would sometimes linger, and we flirted back and forth a bit, but that was the extent of things. Ben and I were always on our best behaviors, projecting our best selves. I remember a time when he stayed past midnight studying, me with my fourth cup of coffee, him with a hot chocolate saturated with hazardous levels of sugar, both of us with papers scattered across my white slatted table. That was the night I thought he'd lean in for a kiss if he wanted one.

But he didn't.

He tells me now that he didn't have the nerve, scared I'd reject his affection. Maybe he was right. Maybe I thought he was too good for me. I had an affinity for bad boys back then, thinking I could save them. I saw Ben as already saved, and, what's more, a little bit of a goody-goody who might be shocked to learn that I could make a bong out of a two-liter even if I did go to Bible Study every week. Still, the clock was ticking, and it felt like we were running out of time to make a play at things. After all, I was graduating that year, and he still had two more to go.

While Ben was trying to muster up the courage to tell me about his feelings, the boy I'd had sense enough to break up with was doing all he could to win me back.

And eventually, he did. Win me back, that is.

He took great pride in reclaiming his lost possession, which was easy for me to misread as love. But we didn't really know all that much about love, I suppose. Not like I do now.

The very day after I had gotten back in my relationship, Ben came to my apartment to spill it all, to finally profess his feelings.

But he didn't. My news of getting back in my relationship hung thick in the air like fog on a bluegrass morning, and he couldn't see past it to tell me. Who could blame him, really? So, I didn't know. He walked away that day, and I moved forward in my relationship.

Ring. Dress. Date.

A week before my wedding, I said these actual words out loud: "I think I may always wonder what a life with Ben Hardin would be like."

FLAG! SOS! MAYDAY!

And yet, "I Do."

And who was there to see it all go down? Ben Hardin, in his siren of a suit with his stunner of a date. Yep. My husband was at my first wedding. Which seems pretty on-brand for me.

And so, we were officially on our separate paths.

Several years passed. We moved to different states, had completely different lives, and all signs indicated that our "almost" would stay just that. The only news I got about him was from his mom if I ran into her in the church lobby on a visit home. Of course, he was doing well. He had a great job, a sweet girlfriend, amazing friends. He couldn't be happier.

With all that in mind, I was surprised to hear that he was moving back to Kentucky.

Around the same time, I found myself moving into an apartment in Lexington and filling out the form to reclaim my maiden name.

At a run-in at church, in the very sanctuary where he first caught my glance, we locked eyes, and I knew: this was our time.

I don't know if I believe in soul mates, but I'm certain that Ben and I, well, we were meant to be a part of each other's story. And so, we set about on our "twice upon a time" with anticipation, excitement, and blissful imaginations toward our happily ever after.

HOT MESS IN THE HOTEL LOBBY

I met her in the lobby of a hotel where our sales team had gathered for our regional meeting. We were both in our late twenties. Within minutes of our introduction, the girl who looked poised and polished in her pressed pantsuit came all the way undone. Her story began to spill out of her as if the pipe of her life sprung a leak and then simply broke apart to let all the despair gush out.

She insisted that I, a perfect stranger, know that her ex-husband had cheated on her with a girl she knew and how now she was left to pick up the pieces of her shattered self. His betrayal of her trust was unfathomable, and it was like she was asking me (or anyone) to help her make sense of the whole thing. She spared no detail—not a one—about her then-husband's late nights and phone calls and meetups with that _____ (enter every choice word you can imagine for mistress).

My eyes had a hard time focusing. Her details held echoes of my own story from my first marriage, but this was her telling of her story. I did not want to superimpose my own experiences onto hers or inch back toward a pain I was doing the work to walk away from. She was a gaping wound wide open, and all my attention needed to be on offering some soothing suggestions of recovery.

"I'm so sorry you are going through all of this. It seems so fresh, and I know it can feel like you'll never be able to come up for air, but—"

She interrupted, "I mean, it's been four years, but can you belieeeeeve him?!?!"

And then, something unexpected happened. "How long?" I asked for clarification. She repeated the timeline. And then something rose up and out of me and onto her. I couldn't believe it, but there I was, and there she was, and the words were coming out uncontrollably and sternly but wrapped in new love for this completely oversharing stranger who was going on and on without end.

"Listen. Is THAT the story you want to tell me? *That* is your story? That happened to you four years ago, and we just met, and *that* is the story you are telling me about yourself? There must be more to your story. There must be more to you. In the time since then, what story have you created for yourself? It sounds like he took enough. Don't just keep handing over your life to him now. What else is there about you that you can find or make or tell outside of that sad storyline?"

She looked stunned. I was shocked myself. But I guess my eyes softened the blow of my words because she didn't punch me in the face. It was like something shorted out in her. Her eyes flickered several times, and her head made a quick side-to-side motion.

"Ummm. Well, I mean . . . I don't really know . . . I mean, I guess I haven't really thought of it . . . or anything . . . or whatever."

"Okay. Well, what if you did? What if you thought of a brand-new story for yourself? What would you want it to sound like?"

I didn't mention how similar our paths were. I'd be damned if *that* was going to be my defining story. It certainly snipped, shaped, and even shredded parts of my heart, but other experiences have been the resurrection to that death. I wanted her to rise from her own embers and write a new story, her redemption story. I want that for everyone, really.

Not much makes my heart swell more than seeing someone set free from the lies that have defined them for too long. So many of us need fresh plotlines injected into those sad stories we tell on loop. Sometimes the things we make sure everyone knows about us are the things that have defined us for too long. Could it be that we hide behind the retelling of old stories to keep from the bravery that it takes to write a new one? Maybe it's time to flip the script.

Eclipsed by the Present

I t's a mantra we hear all the time: Be in the moment.

Right.

Sure.

Like it's that easy.

I'm here with you. And I'm also composing a grocery shopping list. And I can feel the prickles of my unshaved legs, making a mental note to take care of that issue in the shower tonight. Which then makes me wonder, in addition to my neglected hair epilation duties, if that pack of chicken I bought over a week ago is still safe to use. Which takes me back to the grocery list.

All while I sit with you and listen and process.

I'm a second-by-second sojourner, forever traversing multiple time zones.

And why do I do it, when all the gurus and life coaches and mentors shout about the importance of the present? Why, when I agree with their wisdom, do I flit from second to second, sometimes landed here, but also out ahead, but also back behind?

Because the present can cast a long shadow across today.

TRINITY OF TENSE

Mamas are like time travelers, and our passports can let us go between the trinity of tense: past, present, and future.

This morning I am at the coffee shop before school with Celia, who will be thirteen in less than a month. Whenever she suggests we leave early for a stop at The Paddock to hang for a few minutes, *just us*, I do my very best to make it happen. I'll take any sliver of time with her as I'm acutely aware we're always running out of it.

We place our order, and while we wait, a friend notes how tall Celia is, like her daddy. I've only got a half an inch on her at this point. Her long legs walk her to our table, and I watch how she carries herself with ease, poised and confident.

Still, I can't help but interpose this stylish pre-teen with the squishy kid who had cheeks for days, who would cling to my neck as I carried her. The one who's scratchy voice would petition for one more bedtime story almost every night as she nestled into my side, "*Snuggle me, Mommy.*"

Now she's ordering a latte. How did this actually happen?

We trade wins playing slapjack, and she noshes on a warmed strawberry muffin in between games. We talk about who likes who at school and what friends she wants to hang out with soon, and if I like her outfit. I take a sip of my coffee and peer at her over the rim at her sun-kissed face sprinkled with freckles. I wonder who she might be this time next year.

Will she ask me to leave early so we can spend time together? Or will she still want to hang with me at all then?

I'm sure there'll be a time when she doesn't. And then there will be the time on the other side of that one, when— fingers crossed—she does again.

When she's a young woman with a degree or a job or a family or all three, and we're chatting about all the things she's up to. I'll be gushing over her, of course. We'll laugh about how she used to want me to be the best friend kind of mom and how I told her that wasn't my job, but that we would be one day down the road, after we saw this growing up thing through the teenage years.

And there we'll be. In that sweet space.

For now, I try to steady myself in the present, but the alarm of my phone lets us know it's time to drop her off at middle school. This morning, our time together was too short, especially since I experienced it with all three versions of her.

Annie always wakes up after me but before the other two Hardins. This morning, her sleepy eyes appear behind the glass slider doors, and I look up from my laptop to see her smile beam back at mine. This one embodies joy and sharing: it is her superpower. I lay down my computer and motion her to come to me. She shuffles her still-tired feet to the chair and plops down onto my lap.

It's the first day of summer break, so there is no hurry. She presses her cheek against mine, and I place my hand on her other one and nestle her into me. I scratch her back as she stares out over the backyard, almost in a trance.

Her hair is in two-day-old Dutch braids the girl at the salon gave her. I trace them, and we talk about how her hair will be perfectly crimped when she takes them down.

There are pauses of quiet as she comes into wakefulness. In those moments, I travel to a time sitting on our back patio at our first house. She is the smaller version of herself leaning on my chest as we glide in the chair, and I hum as I play with her strawberry blonde sprouts of hair.

My thoughts shift to the wonder of when she'll stop curling up in my lap. When she'll merely sit beside me. Will she still even come to me first thing in the morning and listen to the birds sing with me, or will she dart off to whatever she's into in a few years? She's vowed to live with me forever, but I know better. When will these moments disappear?

I almost tear up thinking about it but am interrupted. She's left the moment, too, but she's looking ahead.

I'm impressed she's lasted a record ten minutes before posing a question. She asks, "Ummmm, Mama. What are we doing today?"

And just like that, the present shifts.

MIX TAPES

Before Spotify playlists, there were mixtapes. Did you make those? The cassette tapes with a carefully compiled collection of songs that were special to you and your friends? We did these for birthday presents, spring break memories, and obviously about all the boys we swore we'd love forever.

My house had no shortage of microphones and recording gear, so I would sometimes make a personal greeting for some of my tapes. Using my most heartfelt and DJ-like tone, it might go something like this:

"Hey, Girl! You are like, one of my best friends in the whole world, and this is a mix just for you with songs that remind me of our friendship! You are like, all that and a bag of chips, and I hope you think this is awesome! You are awesome! Happy Birthday!"

Sometimes these personalized intros would require no less than a dozen takes to get right, but all I had to do was rewind my blooper and record right over it. It was important to make sure the room was quiet because the background noise always seemed to drown out my actual voice, and though the overall sound quality would certifiably suck, my friend would appreciate it.

Only after the best version was captured would I proceed to record a collection of songs from the tape in the other deck or that I ripped off from Casey Kasem's Weekly Top 40. Then I'd line up the sticker label just so and title the mix. "Birthday Mix" or "LYLAS" (Love you like a sister—duh).

It was the actual best!

Sometimes I wish my mouth had a rewind button where, if I said something dumb or sharp or awkward, I could just go back, rewind, and record a more well-thought-out response right over the first shitty one. (Also, I'd like these for everyone else as well. But if there are just one of these buttons in the world of wishes, I've got dibs.)

I'm not saying I'd wear out said button, but I'd definitely use it with regularity.

Sometimes in the moment, our emotions can get the best of us. Or we can make decisions that seem like super choices at the time until exactly four seconds later. Like . . .

— Taking that snarly jab at our partner. (Maybe because we didn't work out the real deal behind the blow.)

— Yelling at our kid.

— Saying "Yes" to something when we should've said, "No, Thank You."

— Announcing a consequence to our kid that we don't want to have to follow through with.

And what if there was a button that not only gave us a second chance at our words but also the stupid things we do? Like . . .

— Getting bangs.
— Mean-mugging the guy who cut you off in traffic before you notice the crying kid in his car.
— Pouring that next glass.
— Making that phone call.
— Eating the whole bag of chips.
— Hitting "Order" on Amazon Prime.

Just to name a few.

Either I'm tired or not focusing or run down or too busy, or whatever, and the die is cast, as my mom would say.

My good sense and kind heart have been eclipsed by my present state of mind or the current state of my heart, and I've blown it. It's out there.

My knee-jerk reaction is a shadow caster, and I'm left in the darkness of the aftermath.

I've hurt someone, overcommitted, been rude, sabotaged myself, overspent, or at the very least jacked up my hair.

And I'd give anything to rewind, start fresh, and make a new imprint of the moment.

Now I have to spend the time unpacking not only what I've said or done but also what in my heart's history may have led to it—and how I can do better in the future.

All because I got caught up in the moment instead of being fully present and rightly oriented, able to maneuver my way through it with more grace.

Since I couldn't reverse and retract, I started to mentally try to press the internal pause button to take a breath so I could give myself time to get my bearings. If I could just mentally press Fast Forward to project the other side of Right Now's bad decision, I may be able to blunt some of the blunders of reaction.

But here's the deal; there is no rewind and re-record. There is no fast forward. So, what is the play when I've blown it?

Apologize. And start again. In the today. In the moment.

It's uncomfortable, sure. It's awkward and clunky. But the tape has already captured my gaff and wishing for it to be erased won't get me there.

That's part of why it's sometimes hard for us to live in the present; we're so busy scrambling to cover the past.

That's part of why it's sometimes hard for us to live in the present; we're so busy scrambling to cover the past.

So, I come back to today. There's no recording over, only moving forward. I apologize to my husband or to my kids for that thing I said. I make the phone call to say sorry, but I actually won't be able to volunteer for that event. I forgive myself for the binge eating or shopping. That's a true mixtape; your greatest hits, your greatest misses, your apologies, and your growth. All captured as the soundtrack of your life.

And this:

Sometimes you have to live with the bangs until they grow out. You might as well learn how to style them for now.

QUESTION QUOTA

Being a mom is the job and joy that you never lay down, check out of, or disconnect from.

But someone just said, "You have reached your QUESTION QUOTA for the day."

Oh.
That was me.
Just now.

Also, it's only 9:47 a.m.

Also, Ben ran point this morning until 9 am.

Meaning I really just arrived on the scene.

Meaning my well of patience should be deeper.

But it's been rapid-fire quizzing since I walked in.

I do not yet know:

> What we are having for lunch.
> What we are doing Friday.
> What we are doing after 4:30 today.
> If we are going to see so-and-so this week. Or this weekend.
> If you will love the after-school activity you are trying.
> If the girl from your third-grade class you used to hang with will be there.
> What time the library opens.
> If they are still on a Covid schedule.
> How many people go to the library instead of buying books.

Also, yes, your outfit is cute, no, you cannot give out your number to that person, and no, I'm sorry, I cannot specifically pinpoint the "thing" you are referring to that we saw on Pinterest "that one time."

The Inquisition. All of this while I'm working across a desk from them in this fresh hell we call Zoom School.

Everything feels interruptive and intrusive. There are literally twenty-nine things on my to-do list, so you can understand that a question quota is entirely reasonable. Also, please note that if they have to stop questioning now, they will not get to ask me math questions. And I hate math. I hated it in the second grade, and I still hate it at forty-five. I certainly don't want to spend seventeen minutes figuring out what 7 x 8 is. Because it's fifty-six every.single.time so you don't need to draw a picture about it and then count up squares and lines that will tell you what I'm telling you. It's fifty-six, fortheloveofGod. You just need to put it to memory like the rest of us have for thousands of years, and then we only have to spend a literal three seconds talking about it because I would ask you, and you would spit it out, and we would be on down the road to anything else but math!!!

Prior to the pandemic, my girls were in traditional school. One result of quarantine is that I am now the center of their social universe. The litany of questions that's part of the mothering experience has kicked into high gear, but it's not just one-sided. I have my own line of questions running parallel to theirs that are begging for answers.

When will life return to normal?
Are we gonna make it financially?
Is there a limit to how many cancellation notifications Airbnb can ping my phone with before it literally explodes?

Can Ben hear the haunting quiet of Main Street as loudly as I can?

Should we be around our parents since we just hung out with friends and we're not sure if we or they or anyone is exposed? And how does all that really work anyway?

How long will our shared expressions be confined to just what we can see from above our masks?

Will this end soon? Ever?

Maybe if we knew when we'd punch the clock on this pandemic, we could better manage it. But since we're swimming in a sea of uncertainty, I've had to give myself a question quota as well. Otherwise, I'll be swallowed up whole in the belly of the whale named Corona.

The two sides of the Covid coin are almost irreconcilable.

One side is heartbreaking and horrific. It tells of the strangling effect of the virus as it scavenges for victims. The ruinous ripple effect on the economy. The psychological impact of social distancing, vacant schools, quieted streets, barren businesses. The perpetual updates, wavering timelines, incessant news. The precariousness of our future.

Turn the coin over and you see the beauty of a Great Global Pause. In the place of chaotic calendars there's intention. I see family dinners, long walks, game nights, camp outs. I hear good conversations, books read aloud, kitchen concerts, Creation singing. I smell my daughters' hair, fresh mowed grass, pots of soup, morning air. I feel them in my arms a little longer, him next to me even though the alarm should be going off, the softness of my favorite cotton shirt against my skin, the Breath of Heaven everywhere. It's not that

Less regimen.

More rhythm.

Less schedule.

More flow.

Less hustling.

More being.

these things were unavailable to see or hear or smell or feel until now. It's that I was sometimes simply too preoccupied to really notice.

Obviously, I am eagerly anticipating the passing of this sweeping devastation. To be spit out of this whale's belly. But I won't be—can't be—catapulted back into the unrelenting pace of Rush and Do. My hope: Less regimen. More rhythm. Less schedule. More flow. Less hustling. More being. And, ahem, less math. And worth repeating again, less math.

ANY GIVEN DAY

On any given day, a chunk of my time can look like this:

I start dinner prep early. It's the only chance to sit down together in case I get called away. I set the oven temperature to 425 for a sheet pan dinner of chicken and veggies. I start the chopping process, and the phone dings. Am I available for a real estate showing in an hour? I call Ben to see if he can pick up Celia from Voice. Finish chopping. Annie walks in with, "Can you play ping pong with me?" We play to ten points because I want to say yes, but no time to make it to twenty today. I might as well switch out the laundry while I'm down here. Season the vegetables. Email dings that the contract my clients submitted has been countered. I call them to discuss our next move. While I'm drafting their electronic signature forms, I toggle through the six other windows open on my screen to make sure there's nothing I need to button up, and I also check to see if the birthday gift I ordered has shipped so that it will be here on time. I kiss Annie and tell her that Daddy and Celia will be home in a few minutes. I can barely breathe when I get in my car, fumigated by smelly socks that were left on my floorboard from the trampoline park. Toss those into the garage. The phone dings with a message from our Airbnb guest saying they can't connect to the Wi-Fi, so I walk them through pulling service from our other spot next door.

I pull into the driveway for the showing, and our cleaning crew calls to tell me that we're out of paper towels and can I get some for the guests arriving tomorrow? Also, hand soap. Stop to get gas, and a lady approaches me; "Do y'all own the event space downtown?" We chat about her daughter's upcoming wedding, and I give her our manager's number. Text dings. Annie has soccer pictures at 5:30 tomorrow night and needs to wear the white jersey that's dirty on the laundry room floor. Set alarm to remind her to wash it. I pull over so I can write an offer on the house my clients just saw, so I'm not distracted by that when I get home. Pull into the garage. Leave my phone in the car. Anyone can wait an hour. Take a deep breath before I walk in to let my body know we're shifting gears. Throw the sheet pan back in the oven to reheat it and fill my plate and my soul at the dinner table with my three favorite people. Get phone from the car, return a client call, and send check-in instructions to the guests coming tomorrow. Roll back inside to see that it's almost time for the girls to dial down for the night. Pile into the bed with my crew for some snuggles and to watch our favorite show. Tuck Annie in with a blessing and squeezes and kisses all over her face. One more text that needs a timely response. Look in on Celia and tuck her in (but make sure not to use those words with her because she's obviously outgrown that, duh). Make tea. Land on the pillow next to B and shape my side in his. We've made it. A collective exhale.

There's an endless well of work to be done around here. And I'm sure I'm not alone in that. I know we've all had planners busting at the actual seams.

And sometimes, the chaos of a present moment can swallow me up. I've had to be clever in creating boundaries around my family and my time, making sure there are sacred spaces carved out when the Do Not Disturb button on my phone stands watch over meaningful moments of ordinary life with my people. I'm certain I've missed a business or social opportunity here or there, but I'm equally sure I've given away a few family moments in trade.

I find in those moments when I'm dialed into who's in front of me, it's the agenda that becomes eclipsed. It shifts behind what's in front of me as I purposely align myself in position with what matters the most. Like . . .

"Mama, I'm having trouble falling asleep. Can you sing to me?" I climb up the ladder to Annie's loft bed and situate myself all snuggled up next to her. I melt into the moment, thankful that she calls for me. I gently pat down the soft shaggy duvet around her and sing her the lullaby my mama's heart wrote the night I brought Cel home from the hospital. I stay for several moments after her deeper breaths tell me she's made it there, to dreamland. But I'm here with her, studying her in her rest. Unconcerned with anything but the sound of her sleeping. And just the magic of her.

OR . . .

It's 8:30 p.m. and Celia walks in the door from being with a friend. She heats up dinner and sits down at the kitchen table. I start to make my to-do list for tomorrow and look up and notice how still she is. I put down my pen and phone and sit with her. "Tell me about tonight, baby." She starts to rattle off "Oh my gosh, Mama" details like only a girl her age does. I listen intently, careful to insert well-thought-out interjections that tell her I'm all-in on our conversation. My eyes widen in unison with her excitement, and we giggle together about this and that. I stroke her back, and she fills in details of her night. We sit until past her normal bedtime because the risk-to-benefit ratio of morning grumpiness is just so worth it. A sweet hug and soft kiss and an "I love you, Mama" as she heads off to her bedroom.

OR . . .

It's a crisp, clear day, and he asks me if I want to go for a Jeep ride. I grab my ball cap and sunglasses and hop in the seat to his right. He fires up the engine and cranks up some Ray LaMontagne. This old 1975 Jeep Wrangler is loud, so there's no talking with words, just the communication of held hands and stoplight glances. We let our whims lead the way and are in no hurry to get back. He in that backwards hat gets me every time. I've been down a lot of roads with this one. Some smooth, some bumpy. Twists and turns for sure. But they all lead us back to each other.

> I've been down a lot of roads with this one. Some smooth, some bumpy. Twists and turns for sure. But they all lead us back to each other.

When I'm free to be captivated by the present moment instead of chained to the minute tick off of my to-do list, life is just better. And there's certainly a balance. It can't all be snuggles and table talks and Jeep rides. But that's the best stuff for sure. I want to make sure not to miss it.

STANDING GUARD

She asks me a question. I mentally answer but realize within a millisecond that I'll shut her down if I reply with what's firing in my brain. I tell my face to soften and ask her to share more with me about what she's thinking. I'm constantly assessing my eyebrow raises, shape of my mouth, tilts of my head. I need to clear my throat but am certain that would be read as disapproval, so I try swallowing several times instead, but without inching my chin forward, a sign that could be seen as holding back words I'm trying not to say. I'm listening intently, working to record every detail so I don't have to go back and ask explanatory questions. My concentration face could be misconstrued as mistrust if I squint my eyes too much, so I labor to make mental notes while maintaining a resting countenance. I interject "uh-huh, yeah yeah" with a bouncy, understanding nod in hopes to come across as not only interested but also calm.

At the end of her disjointed dissertation about her hopeful plans, it takes me a minute to respond. She talks as fast as I do, but I listen at regular tempo, so I'm still a few seconds behind her in the conversation. We have made it to where she's ready for an answer. This time I can offer a sensible yes with a caveat to her want, so we reach a compromise. I'm just so glad about that because I don't have the energy to manage the other side of No right now. I'm still in recovery from the reaction to the earlier one I had to give. I negotiate every nuance of every muscle in my face and each inflection in my voice. We land at a reasonable place of agreement, and she even says, "Thank you, Mama." I return with a light-hearted, "Oh sure, baby. You're welcome. Thanks for talking it through with me." I smile and walk out of her bedroom, shutting the door. I saunter down the hall and across the living room and slide open the glass doors. And then I shut them. And collapse into the chair and let out an exasperated sigh. That was exhausting.

This is life with a teenage daughter.

And this was a "meet in the middle" conversation.

The "nos" can be even harder.

I love the "yes" ones, when the ask is easy and reasonable, but easy and reasonable haven't shown up much on the scene this year.

But I just adore her.

She's so worth it.

I toil with things and tease them out on her behalf because I'm for her.

I "work" on face management because I want her to feel heard and known.

I labor over reactions because I want to keep the lines of communication open with her.

She's my love, and this is where she is right now.

And I'm all up in here with her.

LORETTO

It might be the only one of its kind. The welcome sign for Loretto, Kentucky announces the small area's two greatest landmarks, a convent and a bourbon distillery. This state generally loves both its honey brown elixir and its Heavenly Father, sometimes with equal reverence. People come from miles around to visit both the refuge of serenity at the Sisters of Loretto and the deluge of tastings at Maker's Mark Distillery. I can't help but giggle as I drive by. It is especially ironic considering that there was a time I came to the former to escape the latter.

This particular geography is dense with parochial influence; just down the road from here is another hideaway from the hustle, The Abbey of Gethsemani. I first visited the Abbey in high school with my youth group and can picture that day with such clarity. I found the spare beauty of the unembellished architecture of the monastery calming. There was chanting and liturgy and rituals that were unfamiliar. I remember the afternoon as an invitation to see past the lines of my denomination into another way of experiencing God, at a time when my environment was offering strict instruction to stay within the metes and bounds of our theological plat. Here, God was not ours or theirs. God was God, unbound. The space was encircled within the maple trees on the grounds of Gethsemani where a breeze brushed across my skin, and my wonder of God was renewed. Not the rules or the requirements. Just of God. God was palpable to me for that brief moment.

I found that same sense of Mystery here, in Loretto. I sure didn't expect to when I took my initial trip here years ago. That first visit, I anticipated finding nuns in habits and meek-mannered ladies. I was so wrong.

This is a community of women who "work for justice and act for peace because the Gospel urges." This is a group whose missions place a special emphasis on environmental stewardship, equity for immigrants, the empowerment of women, and disarmament of nuclear weapons. This is a place where the guest information form asks what your preferred pronoun is. This spot is a place of prayer and worship and service, much like you might expect, where sisters live in community—but be sure to note that it's a community of velvet hammers. It's got more of a Joan Baez tenor than a *Sound of Music* vibe. I feel held by the tangible spirit of the women here as well as the mothering heart of God.

I was less than thirty days sober the last time I found my anxious heart here. It's been too long. I have yearned for quiet and craved the cradle of nature to rock a-bye-baby my weary body. Just a little over an hour from home, this place feels like worlds away from the brisk pace of life in full swing. Like with other trips, I can feel my shoulders gradually drop in relaxation the closer I get to the Motherhouse. My soul begins to exhale a little more deeply, even with all the sharp turns in the curvy lanes and the steady showers of heavy rain.

It always comes back around this way for me. I can trace pivotal moments along my "spiritual walk" with each moment I've spent here. I've logged long hours walking through the woods and stumbling through my faith on these grounds. The first time I came as an adult, I filled a journal with questions. Looking back at them, they read with such desperation. I remember thinking that if I could just write enough, I could form words into answers I thought were waiting for me at the end of the last page.

What was the right way to God?
Would God bless me?
How could I become more holy?
What should I be praying?
Was I in or out?

Several iterations of me have found themselves here since then, and all of them have rediscovered how deeply she is loved, has seen the image of God in a new way, and has come to a deeper sense of connection to Spirit.

Today I came with no set agenda, and I wanted to remain fluid in how I spent my time, especially during such a short visit.

I followed the winding gravel path past the deliveries drop off spot and the Rosetta Farm barn, took a left at the Y, passed three simple small cabins, and softly grinned as I saw the sign for my own overnight getaway, the cabin called Grace. I parked and grabbed my bag and hurried up the stairs so I wouldn't get soaked by the cold drops falling off the leaves of the cedar trees above me. Once under the protection of the screened-in porch, I stopped to listen to the sound of the water softly clapping the tin roof.

It's a gear shift coming from our home's swanky mid-century modern feel to the mid-century original of the cabin. Believe it or not, the simplicity of the no-frills dwelling comforts me. Being here has always felt like home on some level. And I'm grateful that there's nothing to keep shiny.

There's a card on the desk from the lady I've been emailing with to make the arrangements for my stay. She welcomes me with a warm note: "As the rain replenishes the earth, so may you, too, be replenished and nourished by the quiet . . ."

I roll out my yoga mat and place a candle in front of me. I watch the fame dance in the gentle breeze for a moment before closing my eyes. Cross-legged, I place my hands on my knees. For so long, I've automatically put my hands palms-down, a much-needed grounding position. Being rooted more deeply these days and feeling wide open to wonder, I chose to place my hands with my palms open, a receiving posture. I draw in a long inhale, noticing the rise of my belly before I slowly release my exhale as well as my grip on the things that are pulling my attention from the moment. A few more deep cleansing breath cycles. And then these words,

"God, will you brush your hand across my cheek today?"

The rain kept falling and the quiet kept me company.

I felt light as I considered how grateful I am that the questions inside, begging for solid answers, didn't fight for my attention. I thought about how many generations of women have come and sat and listened to the rain under this roof over the years, and my imagination spanned the faces of ancient figures way back when to the present.

I felt connected to each one of them. We are all very different and very much the same. I bet we dress differently and eat differently and read different books and write different ramblings and sing different songs. It stands to reason that we likely see the world a bit differently as well. But my hunch is that most of us show up here to meet God. And my guess is that God also shows up to meet them. And me.

Loretto, this setting of refuge, means 'the place of laurels.' A laurel is a plant that symbolizes victory. Too often, I've let hurry and busy and accomplishment symbolize victory to me. Victory over the voices that said I wasn't enough. Victory over rejection. Victory over loss. If I could just achieve enough and hurry enough and be enough, then I could wear a victor's crown. And in addition to all that striving, I tried to medicate the resulting anxiety and frenzy with alcohol, another feature here in Loretto.

But Loretto offers me a victorious experience without any of that now. Here, I'm reminded that the victory is in being present. Being quiet. There's victory in listening. In receiving. In refusing to numb myself. There's victory in feeling all the feelings and surviving them. And it is in Loretto, in this place of victory, that I continue to learn that being with God isn't a race and isn't something that is accomplished; it's something that is absorbed and then diffuses into our very marrow.

"Do not now seek the answers, which cannot be given you because you would not be able to live them. And the point is, to live everything. Live the questions now. Perhaps you will then gradually, without noticing it, live along some distant day into the answer."

— Rilke[5]

Eclipsed by the Future

The promise of tomorrow is that it will surely evade us. Still, we insist on spending so much time there. Sometimes I let it rob me of today's sweetness and yesterday's nostalgia. Psychologists talk about how people often live in the past or in the future. And future-casting can be one of my strongest diversions from the present.

Left unchecked, my predictions and worries and expectations about the future can keep today dim, a washed-out version of where I want to be, where I hoped to be by now, and where I think I should be.

HER SONG

She walks from the sidelines of the school gym floor to nearly center court, where the microphone is.

She plants her feet and stands tall.

Her fingers are interlaced, and her hands are resting in front of her.

She looks calm and certain.

My shoulders are tense.
My breath is shallow.
My stomach is in knots.

You see, I am only partly there. Part of me has traveled back to 1984 to the sanctuary of First Christian Church. It's the place where I forgot the words to my cherub choir solo in front of the whole church. Losing the thread of the lyrics in front of my family and community at that tender age tipped a mute button in my psyche; I didn't sing again publicly for years and years. That memory is seared into my mind, and my body registers angst that the same thing could happen to Annie.

The music starts and I'm brought back to the Now, in the gym of Painted Stone Elementary.

Annie's mouth opens.

She begins to sing.

I'm sweaty.
Nervous.
Anxious.

Will she forget the words?
Like I did?

I wish I could tell you that I was able to finally relax into the enjoyment of her performance. But I couldn't. Sure I savored the iPhone recording of this precious moment, but I missed the pulp of it in the present.

I interposed my past fears into each note of her song. I was one step ahead of each word, cheering her on to make it to the end. Frantic that she might not.

But she didn't need me to. She needed me to just breathe. Actually, by the looks of it, she didn't need me at all. She was just doing her thing and doing it boldly and beautifully, and sure, it'd be a shame if I missed it, but she was rolling along either way.

And I must note that if she had forgotten the song altogether in front of her school, I would've scooped her up and loved her up. This wasn't about an on-point execution that had her collecting compliments. I was all tangled up in her heart's wiring, not short-circuiting over this four-minute moment. You know, like when it happened to me.

Sometimes I mentally water the weeds of my own wounds and imagine them growing around the blooming blossoms of my girls just because they're planted in the same garden as me.

I was worried that the same seed of self-doubt that planted itself into me would have an opportunity to plant in Annie's spirit and keep her song buried deep inside of her for a long time. I was concerned that her post-song confidence would diminish if she wasn't pleased with her performance. That she would be enveloped in that same embarrassment that sealed me in all those years ago. That she would be covered in the same shroud of shame that covered me all those years ago.

I had literally made all of that worry storm inside of me for n o t h i n g.

Because she is not me, and this is not my song.

She is Annie, and this is her song.

And she sang it beautifully. Without missing a beat.

MEDLEY OF MEMORIES

Her words were a medley of memories and an assortment of observations, only some of them real.

They brought her a tray of puréed food and thickened water. She kept asking for a drink from the tap but was told her dietary restrictions wouldn't allow it. The question struck me—what happens inside of a person who has started several businesses, raised five children in her blended family, and maintained an antique booth up until just last week when they get to a point of thirst and can't even have a single cup of water?

Her dignity thinned as she asked again and was denied.

The room was full of sounds that jolted me. NASCAR on the television, alarms from leads she was wearing, doors sliding open and shut with nurse check-ins.

I traced my fingers to calm my own anxiety as Ben adjusted her blanket.

I made eye contact with and offered warmth to each caretaker, the nurse who'd earned the nickname The General, and the social worker wondering about our plan on the other side of her hospital stay.

I tried to hide the fear in my eyes. For her. For her boys, making hard decisions on her behalf. For me, as I imagined myself in that bed one day. Is this what the bustling life I'm leading now turns into one day?

I'm not afraid of death.
But dying?
Terrified.
Horrified.

Is this how it ends?
What if it is?
Have I done enough?
Will I have by then?
What else do I want to do?
See?
Change?
Try?
Experience?
Taste?
Be?
Explore?
Time is running out.

I want to make sure that whenever my vibrancy is eclipsed by the years of diminishing, I have a lifetime of love and adventure to bask in. That way, if I lose half of my mind, there will still be plenty of beautiful memories in which to reside.

The girls.
How will they manage?
Will I be a burden?
Can they care for me? Us?
What decisions will they have to make?
Oh, my sweet girls. I hope you never see me this way.

And Ben. My eyes tear up as I see him clasp and gently squeeze his mama's hand. Will he be holding mine as I lay there, or will I be nursing him as he points to someone who isn't there?

I've always just let myself imagine that if I lost my memories, it would be like *The Notebook,* and he'd read our story back to me, the best parts twice. And then he'd curl up with me, and we'd fade away together, holding each other.

But for now, I'll hold onto him as he holds onto her, and we will just get through today, together.

GURU

Four hundred and thirty-two words. That's all I had written worth saving over about twelve hours. I was trying to write the introduction to this book. Concerned that it would be contrived or overproduced, I kept drafting stuff I didn't like. And then my fingers stopped moving altogether. It was excruciating. Besides, I was on the clock. My hotel checkout was at eleven, and my schedule back at home was sure to barrage me the minute I hit the door. This time was carved out, and I couldn't perform.

What if I couldn't get it done?

The pressure mounted as the minutes ticked on, and I felt the weight of failure as I imagined the email I'd have to send saying I couldn't deliver.

Ben and the girls called. They were in the Jeep and headed out for burgers at our favorite spot. I heard delight in their voices and freedom in their tones, and I was jealous. I told them about my struggle and confessed I was near the point of tears. Everyone chimed in with words of encouragement like, "You got this, Mama!" and "Baby, I know you've got it in you. I know you can do it." And I belabored the point with my whining and despair.

And then Annie piped up.

"Everyone, listen up. Daddy, turn the radio down. I've got something to say. Are you listening?"

We all acknowledged that she had our attention.

"Mama, the Spirit is trying to tell you something, and I can't believe I have to tell you this." She was scolding but soft. "You have to stop trying. You're trying to go towards it, but it will come to you. Go for a walk or a run, get some good food, and have fun. And then you will find it. That's how it happens."

She's ten.

My youngest and sweetest teacher. My guru.

At her insistence, I put down the laptop and tucked away the dozen or so scraps of paper with pen-scratched ideas. I went for a walk, had a nice dinner—and bought an overpriced t-shirt to boot.

And just as Annie said, the words came once I stopped darting toward them. As soon as I dropped into Now and moved back into myself instead of imagining the missed deadline or projecting my future flop, my mind opened up. And actually being in Now instead of striving so hard for Then got me from Here to There.

> **"You have to stop trying. You're trying to go towards it, but it will come to you. Go for a walk or a run, get some good food, and have fun. And then you will find it. That's how it happens."**

The same can be said about so many things.

I've had seasons of life when I've run so hard toward something ahead of me that I missed the lessons and beauty that Now came to teach me.

I've falsely projected upcoming doom so as to press and hold my heart's panic button until I've drained the joy of Today.

And what's more, sometimes I've sprinted toward something in the future just to outrun today, thinking that There would be better than Here and the unfinished work of Here wouldn't follow me There.

And what about when I've run past where I am toward something that isn't even there? We're all familiar with that illusion called Perfect Timing, when all the stars align for you to have a baby, lose weight, start that project, quit that job, get sober, try that class, start exercising. I've gotten snagged here more often than I can remember.

It's easy for me to be engulfed by the future. To let catastrophizing about what Will Be deprive me from the What Is. Or even, on the other hand, being so overwhelmed by the steps needed to get to a better way for myself in the future that I stay stuck in the same predictable patterns of today.

I remember being taunted by predictions of what life would look like for me if I stopped drinking. I would lie in bed and try to conjure up positive portrayals of a sober me just before I passed out. I couldn't access her.

The false narrative on loop was that I would never be fun again, life would never be enjoyable, no one would want to hang out with me. I couldn't picture myself even doing life's daily details without drinking.

How would I bear to make dinner without a cocktail to sip on? And then after dinner, what do you do then? Just like, hang out? Like, without a drink?

When the kids were trying my patience, I'd just have to manage that without "Mommy Juice?"

And what about being with friends? How could I possibly get through a dinner, a girls' night, a campout, a party? And vacation would be impossible.

Obviously, I wouldn't be able to sing. Sing without something to take the edge off? Forget it.

Plus, it's summer—Cocktails on the deck!

Or it's winter—Wine by the fire!

And how could I even consider getting sober while our family home was an Airbnb and I was living out of a suitcase most every weekend?

Packing up my life and relocating it every weekend and actually fully feeling the severance of that?

God. No. Way.

But then, instead of trying to imagine a whole life without drinking, I just wondered what just one day would look like. And it seemed like I might have some kind of chance at that. I think that's why the recovery mantra of "one day at a time" has come to mean so much to me.

> **When I can't imagine a better tomorrow, I can't create one for myself.**

When I can't imagine a better tomorrow, I can't create one for myself. It's not that thinking of the future throws me into panic. It's the kind of future I allow to take shape in my mind. If I forecast doom, gloom, or boredom, it gives a backwash of shadow onto today. When I can project promise and progress, I can better trust that the steps to get there are worth taking. And sometimes, it's about letting go of any expectations for just a moment so I can catch my breath. It's about trusting the words of the Spirit through my mini-guru and letting what I need come to me.

MAMA SAGE

I'm smarter than I used to be. More patient, too. And even still funnier because I can laugh at myself now. Getting older is just way better than I ever assumed it would be. Sometimes I get giddy when I imagine Mid-Sixties Me. I'll be rocking a scarf around my turkey neck, talking too loudly, and will likely be as filterless as the Camels I smoked in college. I hope that I will also be more gracious for my shadow selves of yesteryear and especially tender toward those young women and mamas just finding their way. And eighty-year-old me, the one I call Mama Sage? All the more beautiful in my ways, thanks to the lessons I will have learned through past experience. I'll trust myself even more then, have a steady expectation of the positive, and know better what does and doesn't matter as much.

Sometimes I wish the older version of ourselves could raise our kids. That way, we'd be freer to love and raise them with wisdom that only comes with a wealth of wrinkles. How lucky my girls would be with a much wiser, consistently calmer sage of a mama like the one I could be years from now. If I could interpose my now energy level with my then emotional intelligence? Wow. That'd be something.

Because we default to what we know, how much better to have the years to recalibrate our defaults after Teacher Time has taught us so much more?

I have to shake my head at some of the things I thought were so paramount when the girls were small. I'd get bent out of shape about things like eating fast food or staying up too late, or watching more than one hour of television. Listen, nobody thrives on crap food and no sleep, and too much tech. My mind hasn't changed about that. But likewise, nobody thrives with a mom who's in angst about one Happy Meal, a missed bedtime, or a long stint on the iPad at the grandparents' house.

And, honestly, was I really concerned about *them*? Or was I busy managing my mom rep as the one whose kids ate lots of veggies and got great sleep and spent tons of time outside? (Also, that isn't really a question.)

As a new mom, I thought I'd make a good guess about what my children might want or need. It's so silly to think about now. They are so different from who I thought they would be. It took me a while to learn to see what naturally flowed from them and then roll with that.

I was so concerned about channeling the right stuff into them early on. I thought everything was going to mark the end of their innocence. I wanted to shelter them. I wanted to control their little worlds with all my micromanaging-mama-bear might. And if I couldn't control their whole world, I'd at the very least control their bedrooms. I was a super neat kid. Clean lines have always traced a footpath to peace for me. But my kids aren't on that route. And until recently, the conditions they choose to live in gave me anxiety. But after getting bent out of shape for so long, I finally decided to flex. You see, I had an epiphany. I have a house with doors, so I can just close them. And then, if need be, I can pretend that there is order behind said doors. Me easing up on them about that has alleviated stress for all of us.

I had a whole list of things to avoid for them, mostly rooted in what I thought would darken their bright little hearts. Like Halloween and Harry Potter. These landed under the category of witchcraft, and so, of course, it was a gateway to demons. Letting my girls step foot into that kind of world when they were old enough would be opening up that gate. Thank God for both me and them, I wised up to their wonder. This past year, we took the girls trick-or-treating in two neighborhoods. (You know, we gotta make up for the five weird years we hid in my mom's basement while every kid they knew was out having fun.) Also, we've run the whole course at Hogwarts now. Sage Mama never would have worried about these things!

Public crying also used to freak me out. One kid is in the cart melting down, which signals the other that there is something to be upset about, and before you know it, there's a chorus of cries. Now, I know that other moms really don't care. They are just grateful it's not their baby that they have to soothe or their toddler having a tantrum on the floor. And actually, no one really cares.

Once upon a trip to the grocery, one of mine lost her mind because I said no to her insistence that I get her gum. Like full on lay on the floor, kick and scream tantrum. I bent down to where she was and said, "We don't do that in our family, so when you're done here by yourself, we'll be over here by the door." I stepped over her, and she wailed for what seemed like twenty minutes but was more likely just a few. The neighboring shoppers became the audience to my plight, and I was literally sweating as I imagined their eyes glued to this debacle of what was just supposed to be a quick grocery run. Just as I stood there literally sweating, an older mama came and stood beside me. She said, "I'll stay here with you. I know it's hard to do the right thing, but you're doing it, sister." Before I knew it, a red-faced daughter made her way to me. I thanked my mama-partner, took the little hand that reached for mine, and walked to the car. I was so embarrassed until that wiser and more experienced mom breathed life into my wilting will.

I'll admit it; I was proud that I didn't give in to her demands. But I'm not always that calm with resolve, especially with an audience. I used to be constantly concerned about the girls' behavior in public. We all have versions of these stories.

You're pulling up into the church or school parking lot or the friend's driveway, chanting the mantra, "You better be especially good here. You better be nice to so and so. You better behave yourself."

When we do this, we're teaching them posturing and, what's worse, it's mostly to make us look good. I'm not saying we don't have standards. Of course, we do. But I don't want my girls to step into a facade of ever-polished behavior at the expense of truth-telling and showing up as themselves. When we think about it, none of us really do.

When I wasn't busy making sure my girls cleaned up messes and learned our Hardin way of doing things, I was doing what I could to make sure they had storybook childhoods.

I remember I'd host playdates early on; I'd bake fresh muffins sans every single allergen on the forbidden foods list between all the kids. I'd clean the house before everyone showed up, fluffing couch pillows on the way to answer the door. I'd make a Walmart run for supplies like craft projects and board games. I still love having a gaggle of girls hanging at our house now, and I still make an effort to create some entertainment for my kids. But more often than not, they hear, "I'm not here to entertain you. She can come over, but you're on your own for fun. Your friend is your fun." When my kids complain that they are bored, my response is, "You just described the bigger part of the 80s for your daddy and me. Be resourceful and make something happen for yourself."

We all long to give our children the world. It's a natural inclination for us mamas. But sometimes, I think we set up childhoods that are so spectacular that they'll never be satisfied in adulthood. Mama Sage would have known never to vacuum before kids come over. That's clearly a post-party chore. And she'd know that a kid really just wants to be loved. Sure, sometimes that can look like over-the-top grand gestures, but mostly it's just about being with them, listening to their ideas and (long-winded, disjointed) stories, sticking a note on their bathroom mirror, or watching their favorite YouTuber with them.

Look, no one escapes childhood unscathed. We all have wounds. As parents, we're bound to wound our kids, sometimes without even realizing it. Sure, it'd be great to bring up our babes with the insight our future holds for us, but it's just us and here and now. Since the Now Me is the one that's here to raise these girls, I've done the best I can to distill things through the future filter. I ask myself, "Will this matter in a year? Five? Or even in ten minutes?"

I've realized that a lot just doesn't.

What does hold true for Now and for Then: Love. A ton of love. The unconditional kind. Fierce love for them. Fierce love for myself so that I can better love them. And hopefully, that love will curb their checklist of Mom Faults in the coming years. Or at least make those faults more palatable because they know that I've loved, loved, loved them with everything I've got.

Eclipsed by a Shadow

T hings in our lives can cast a long, influential shadow over who we are versus who we think we are supposed to be. Maybe it's that you have a wildly talented family member, and so you think you should be too. Or that you can never measure up, so you don't try. Maybe it's the shadow of a hurt in your partner's life, something they don't ever want to experience again. And so, you find yourself avoiding certain conversations or topics because the reach of that shadow still shimmers. Maybe it's something from your parent's life, something they don't want you to ever experience, and so they tuck you away in the shade, trying to protect you. Maybe it's the shadow of something that should be good, but it means you feel like you have to live up to what someone wants in *their* life. It's ephemeral and translucent, but it's still there, an influence that propels you and shapes you.

Those shadows show up for all of us if we know where to look.

LIFESAVER

It came up regularly, but it was always unexpected. Even years after my brother Brent's death, people would offer their condolences to my parents. Their intent was compassion, maybe as if to say, "I haven't forgotten your pain." And I think that's important. But still, it spliced the lightness of a moment with the weightiness of reality, and the emotional strands of that braid seemed like they'd always be woven tightly together. A fun or frivolous moment could not belong to my mom and dad for long without being drawn back into their grief.

One of those moments is frozen in my memory.

We were at a post-church potluck with other families. The southern America signature scents of meatloaf and blackberry cobbler perfumed the air. I was six or seven years old, a helmet of a bob haircut framing my face, a butterscotch candy coating my tongue. The din of adult conversation, with such titillating topics of *we're having to have the roof repaired again* and *I've got to have the recipe for your macaroni salad*, created a hospitable tenor. I can still picture my mom. She was wearing a tweed blazer with a white blouse underneath. Her hair was dark then, before she started sporting highlights. It was the outfit and hairstyle she wore in our church pictorial directory, and I think of her in it often.

A woman approached my mother. I was at my mom's left side, swaying with impatience, already bored with all the adult conversation and niceties. The noise of the room faded as this woman tilted her head to the side and began offering words of comfort about Brent. Some part of me knew she was going to say something about my brother, even before the words were out. I strained to listen, always looking for clues about

Brent, always wanting to find some way to know just a little bit more about him. There was a comment made about the interesting timing of Brent's death and my birth, only months apart. A comment about God's perfect plan. I always thought that was a weird thing for people to say. How is there ever perfection in any timing when a child dies? In response to the woman's comments, my mom put her hand on my shoulder and recounted, "Yes, she saved our lives, really."

They both looked at me with adoring eyes.

I stopped swaying.

I saved their lives?

It's hard to know how deeply a word will embed into the heart of someone.

Some little girls may have worn that statement as a badge of honor. Or maybe would have just heard it as an exaggerated but kind comment and moved on down the road, never giving it another thought.

But for me, it was a life sentence.

I saved their lives.

So, I guess I needed to keep on saving them.

I needed to make sure I was enough to curb their sorrow.

To be the worth of two children.

To make up for the one they lost.

I needed to keep outrunning the shadow of their grief.

No one intentionally handed me that yoke. I just took it to bear.

Years later, I had a conversation with my sweet Mama about that remark. Of course, she didn't even remember saying it. After all, to her, it wasn't an announcement. It was a well-meaning acknowledgement. But we unpacked it together.

She understood that she might have, in fact, thought that. In a sense, I did save their lives. I kept them busy. Changing diapers, feeding me, teaching me to walk, and all the other countless demands a growing baby has. There was little time to just fall all the way apart. To absolutely collapse under their crushing suffering. In the best sense, I was a distraction from their sadness. They were crazy about my towheaded big brother, but being older, he didn't have the same logistical needs that I did. He could put on his own shoes and grab himself a snack and play with the neighbors. But I needed them for survival. And, as it turns out, they needed me for the same.

SILENT SONGBIRD

I'd been up since before my alarm rang, roused by the vocal scales my daddy was singing in the hall bathroom just down from my bedroom. This was a regular occurrence, and though I preferred to be sleeping, it was a sweet wake-up call.

Our taste in music finds little intersection, but I could listen to my daddy's tenor voice all day. And because music emits from his pores, I often do. There's a black-and-white picture of him hanging in the hall at the bottom of our steps. He is singing lead but sharing the microphone with the rest of his quartet. He's got a smile behind his eyes, and his signature pointed index finger in the air. You see, he's as much of a storyteller as he is a singer, and the rise of his finger lets you know that you need to listen to what's coming next.

My mother's picture hangs next to his, a rendering of her on stage portraying the main role of Julie in the University of Kentucky's musical *Carousel*. I often stop to admire this image of her. She then stands next to me to remind me that she had to drop down one of the choruses to an octave lower during the performance, thanks to her former affinity for Winston cigarettes. She has a hard time just basking in my awe of her.

On rare occasions, I got to hear my parents sing together, usually at church for "special music." Each time they approached the stage, my Grandmom glanced at me, squeezed my hand, and reminded me, "I just love to hear your mother and daddy sing." Though Mama's voice is more trained and formal than Daddy's, the melodies they make marry beautifully.

Grandmom Mathis got to hear her fair share of my brother Lewis's music, too. Her basement was the setting of his regular band practice. This meant that in her eighties, she turned down her Bing Crosby cassette to hear Lewis and his band crank out the likes of Pink Floyd and the Rolling Stones. My brother embodies music. From the time my parents gave him a guitar for his fifth birthday, it's been as much a part of him as his actual limbs. Watching him play is like watching him teleport to another realm, and you are invited. I'm mesmerized by both him and it.

Inches away from where my mom and dad's pictures are on display, there is a pictorial homage for my brother. One framed newspaper article headlines him as Shelbyville's "Music Man." I believe my first memory of Lewis is of him playing guitar . . . or maybe it is just such a part of him that I can't separate the two, the man from the music.

How did they all get so brave?

What happened to my dose of courage?

"Do you sing?" It's a question I am often asked by any number of people after someone hears one of my family members perform.

The truth is, I lost my confidence singing when I was nine years old, when I forgot those words to my cherub choir solo in front of the whole church congregation. Besides, my family musicians were incredible, and I was afraid I would never match up. So, I didn't really try. Digging deeper, as the hero child, I didn't give myself to music the way I wanted to because it was "Lewis's thing." I just let it be his.

Still, I have my own musical picture on the wall at the bottom of the steps from a school play I was in. I walked down the choral room my senior year of high school and stumbled upon auditions for the school musical. Shocked by my spontaneity and with no time to work up anxiety over the audition, I went out for a role. Turns out my speaking voice was low enough to be believable as a twelve-year-old boy and high enough to hit the notes in his musical score, so I was granted the role of Monroe in *Aesop's Fabulous Fable Factory.*

The gig was not as threatening as the solos I would never go out for in Show Choir, where I was more than content to let my voice blend into the chorus. This play was a traveling performance to elementary and middle schools, so I was told none of my peers would see it.

That performance as Monroe wrapped up my music career, as far as I was concerned.

After graduation, I never really considered singing, but I always dreamed about it. I didn't reach for it like it was attainable but instead imagined what it might feel like to be brave enough to belt out the music in my heart. I kept my song inside of me for the next seventeen years.

I'd be at the front row of my big brother's gigs as he turned his gift into his life's work and played regularly. My dad still sang beautifully and frequently. He sang The Lord's Prayer at dozens of weddings and funerals in town, along with performances at local shows and church services. I recall being envious of that. Not of him. Just of his ability to let it out. My mom would share her gift from time to time, but those moments had longer spaces of quiet in between. I missed hearing her sing. Almost as much as I missed singing myself.

Sometimes I would forget how free I could feel until my house was empty, my music was loud, and my inhibitions were gone. I believe we all sort of have a Life Soundtrack of signature moments, where in private we belt out our favorites, away from the hearing of others, no stage fright, no shame. I'd serenade the air with all the best ones, the tunes from that college spring break trip and that other one from prom. I'd throw in some country favorites and a little blues.

But it wasn't for anyone to hear. It was just for me. Not for an audience.

It wasn't until I had Celia, until my own empowerment became tangible through her birth, that I wondered what else I might be capable of. And so, I began to imagine myself singing for more than just my shower or sun visor. Every time I pictured it, I'd get a little shaky. And project that I'd forget the words. And envision the crowd staring silently back at me with winced expressions if I hit a wrong note. Even still, at the insistent prompting of my emerging confidence that assured me we'd be okay, I eventually made my way to the stage. With all the nerves, but with a newfound grace, I stepped back in front of the microphone. I led worship at church. I sang with my brother at some of his gigs. Eventually we even started a band together. The wings of this unsung songbird began to unfurl. I finally found my voice.

ALLI

I just wanted to see what it felt like.

It would be my second summer stay at Camp Hollymont in North Carolina. This time I was spending two weeks. Fourteen days with fresh faces and new experiences in a serene setting.

When I approached the registrar's table, I picked up my name tag and squealed with delight when I saw what was on it: Alli Mathis.

Months before when we were filling out the thick packet of camp paperwork, I somehow convinced my mom to let me use a shortened version of my middle name, Allison, instead of my given name, Melinda, which I'd never been crazy about. And so, this year, I was going to camp in the new and improved identity of Alli.

At first, it felt awkward. Would people know it wasn't my actual name? Nope. They had no reason not to believe the printed title on the tag. So, there I was, in a different state with a different name. I felt like one of those people in the movies who reach for a pseudo passport when they need to make a clean break.

And I wanted a clean break.

I wondered; if I had a new name, would that make me feel different all the way around? Who could I be as the character of Alli? Maybe her house was light and airy with parents that knew no grief. Maybe she scored high on the standardized tests at school. Maybe both of her brothers were alive and well, and the letters they would write to me at camp would be for Alli. And when my name was called out at mess hall to come get those letters, the camp counselors would say, "Letters for Alli!" Was it possible that Alli didn't hyperventilate at swim meets out of nervousness? And what if Alli wasn't afraid to try things that would usually intimidate Melinda? I bet Alli wasn't exhausted from trying to keep everyone happy!

At first, I loved introducing myself with my new identity. It was exhilarating!

"Hi! I'm Alli!" (Cue my awkward face, like simply telling them my "name" held all the significance for them that it did for me.) Even still, it felt like a production, and I was both writing and directing the script. The opening curtain speech was confident. But the actual follow-up was just a B-grade performance.

Really, past the "nice to meet yous," everything else was familiar. I hadn't thought through creating an entirely new self; I'd only pondered what a new name might do for me, not what I might have to do for it. I was just naive enough then to think a name switch could translate into more than it actually did. It was my first realization of the expression, "Wherever you go, there you are."

As it turns out, during share time around campfire circles, Alli's family was just like mine. We lived in the same small town, were in the same grade, and had the same interests. I just couldn't pull the trigger on a total ruse. And truth be told, I didn't really want to be fully emancipated from myself. I just wanted to make some amendments.

What I discovered is that some things you just get and you have to keep. Like the darker details of my family's tragic loss and all its ripple effects. But some things are yours to change. Like not letting your nerves keep you from auditioning for the talent show. (My band of newfound friends and I gave a heckuva lip-sync performance of Bon Jovi's "Livin' on a Prayer," complete with my "guitar" solo on a tennis racquet. Yes ma'am, we sure did.) Also, Melinda never took dance classes, but Alli signed up for both jazz and ballet at camp and loved every turn and twirl. Plus, when a boy made fun of Alli for a scar on her leg that Melinda had always been self-conscious about, Alli shook it off. Maybe Alli could pack some of that bravery into her suitcase and take it home with her to Melinda? Was that possible?

In the end, that's what happened. A little mischief not only made for unforgettable camp memories but also yielded some unexpected emotional metamorphoses. It was an odd onramp, but I'd likely do it all the same again. Deciding to imagine another me helped me step into more of the me I wanted to be. It paved a way down a path I had been hesitant to walk. At the same time, it gave me an appreciation for the fragility of the girl I was going home to. I had no interest in berating her for her sadness or apprehensions. After all, I had a front-row seat to understand it all. But the door had opened, just a crack, where I could see an opportunity, through Alli, to show Melinda just what she was actually made of, the stronger stuff that was in her marrow. It was a lesson that would take many more years and mistakes and messes to take hold. But I'm endeared to Alli for all that she taught me.

Alli, this one's for you.
Thank you.
Thank me.

PERSPECTIVE

She was the winner. From spelling bees to valedictorian and just about every academic award in between you could think of. At some point, I suppose I just resigned myself to the fact that she'd be the one standing with the plaque or paper announcing her achievement, so what was the point of reaching?

She killed it. I didn't even consider auditioning for the solo after hearing her sing it for our choir director. She was self-assured and poised, and her boldness gave a depth to the song few girls our age could capture. I was blown away. And walked away from even trying.

She was striking. With womanly curves and long legs and thick locks of blonde hair down to her lower back, one couldn't help but notice her. I was her "meh" tagalong to the college parties and bars, always answering questions about her availability to clumsy boys taken aback by her confident stride and sex appeal. I'm not sure I ever complimented her.

She was hysterical. There was never a dull moment with her. Her wit was well-timed and without end. Instead of joining in with my good humor, I just laughed along as an audience member of her life, telling myself "funny" was taken. It belonged to her.

She was a boss. Self-assured with swagger to boot, she owned whatever room she was in. She seemingly assumed everyone would listen to her and follow her lead, and that's just what we all did. Even my best ideas paled next to the delivery of hers, so I went along with her ways. And eventually stopped contributing except to echo her ideas.

She was a writer. Her words dripped like the honey of poetry onto the page, and I was swept up in each of the pieces she shared with the class. My words fell so flat next to hers. So, I just stopped sharing mine.

I was raised to think there's only so much pie on the talent plate, and you've got to fight for your piece. But my insecurity wasn't all that interested in throwing elbows, and so I mostly just left the pie on the plate and walked away hungry.

I've had to learn to change my outlook and my response. What if it's not an opportunity drought with only so many resources to share, but rather a chance to celebrate, encourage, and take envy off the table? Here's what the dialogue looks like when that is true:

She is the winner! It is her league, and she is slaying it! I grab my pom-poms and cheer her on! Her victory rallies me to aim at my own targets. I hug and high-five her with pure celebration in my heart. Go her!

She's killing it! I am thrilled to see her unleash her gift of song! She takes us on a journey, connecting us to the story of her music. And what bravery that took! Amazing!! My hands hurt from clapping so loud! And then I take the stage to share my own song.

She is striking! I have to tell her I notice. I approach her and offer, "Gosh, I'm sure you hear this a lot, but I mean, you're just breathtakingly beautiful!" I take a note of her lip gloss for future reference and offer her a full smile.

She is hysterical! I love how deeply I belly laugh with her, and our banter is without pause. We trade quick quips and are sore from cackling so hard. I keep telling her she needs her own comedy act. I'd be in the front row!

She is a natural leader! I commend her and take notes from her playbook. I elbow others beside me and point to her accomplishments, gushing about her go-getter goal-smashing success. I'm so proud of and thrilled for her!

She is a writer! I treasure the wisdom of her words and am constantly impressed with her natural ability of expression. I encourage her to write more—a post, a blog, a book! Anything! Her texts even read like a song and, in fact, make me a better writer, opening channels in my soul to explore with my own words.

I remember my mom telling me growing up, "There will always be someone smarter than you, and you'll always be smarter than someone else." (Also useful when you insert: prettier, more accomplished, more talented, more all the things.)

I never really got that then.

I felt defeated when someone else soared instead of encouraged by it. Now, seeing other women excel fuels me.

It's part of the evolution of self-compassion that allows us to fully accept ourselves next to someone else's success or win. To understand that their radiance does not mean we're dull or tarnished. It's not that fellow woman that makes us slide behind her brightness. It is a willful walk behind it. Likewise, it is a conscious effort to come back out from behind it.

And then where do you go from there?

Well, there is no need to race out in front of it.

That's the lie we've been told.

Outpace.

Outrun.

Outdo.

We as women need each other.

Let's get beside each other.

Next to each other.

Alongside each other.

We are the best versions of ourselves when we share the spotlight so that there is no spotlight at all, only abounding brilliance cast across all of us wholly being ourselves.

ALL OF US

Being from a small town, I used to think the "great big world" was Louisville. Maybe Kentucky. My sweet budding naïve mind thought right here was all there was. Without any ill intention, I naturally divided people as "us" and "them." Like people from here and then everyone everywhere else. I saw my traditions, beliefs, and mindset in light only of my own experience. My vision of a bigger world was shrouded by lack of encounter with otherness.

What a beautiful gift, to learn the story of another.

As I got older, I had the privilege of meeting and cultivating relationships with many of "them." People who looked differently, spoke differently, thought differently, and so on. What a beautiful gift, to learn the story of another. To hold space for the sacredness of their way. To learn about their responses, reactions, and revelations about life. Soon the lines of separateness began to blur and eventually fade away. Instead of "us" and "them," I discovered that it's really just "us."

"The one thing we all have in common is our differences."

I recently read this quote that was painted along the stretch of a wall in a faraway city. I stopped my hustling pace and read it out loud with my daughters. During our trip, I continued to recite it and point out the beautiful contrasts in the faces and places we encountered. It's exceedingly important to me that Celia and Annie hold sacred the connectedness of all people. I pray that they honor the commonalities as well as the diverse distinctions that thread through the tapestry of humanity.

There was one moment along our way that painted the perfect picture of the juxtaposition of likeness and difference. We were making our way through customs in the Newark airport. The girls were inquisitively studying the lines of people, noticing with awe the varied shades of skin, the indigenous garments, and the array of languages. On one side of us, there was an Orthodox Jewish family. The peyos, the traditional long curls the men wear just in front of their ears, were of particular interest to my curious companions. On our other side was another beautiful family and the girls were reminding each other about why they could only see the mother's eyes as her head and face were both covered. A few paces in front of us stood a guy who looked like a 1990s rapper with his flat-billed Raiders hat and gold chain securing a pendant the size of a hood ornament. And just behind us was a German family excitedly discussing . . . well, something I couldn't understand, but from the tone and body language, it seemed wonderful.

So here we were, in a cultural casserole of sorts, all blended in this same rectangle. And then, in what seemed like an orchestrated moment from heaven, I noticed the sweetest thing. Four babies started making cries and coos that signaled their parents' attention. And in synchronicity, four fathers swooped down to comfort their babes. A universal instinct of love. A father caring for his child. In that moment, these men each had an expression of softness and comfort. One swept his long curl from his face to meet eyes that needed him. Another tucked his chain under his shirt to keep it from his son's grip. And in that moment, they were all just fathers.

I stood there and let the lesson that everyday humanness was teaching me sink in. It literally made me weep as I was reminded again of how we are all connected.

But it's all too easy to stop seeing where we're all connected, and simultaneously to also stop seeing the ways in which we are divided. I thought in my early adult years that we had made such strides overcoming racism and polarization in this country. Now I see that I had simply stopped shining a spotlight on it. And when the spotlight is removed from our prejudices and judgements and exclusions of those we see as different from us, our fellow humans in the travel concourse that is life become shrouded once again in 'otherness,' and the plight of divisions slips to the shadows.

I think about the echo of our ethnocentric experience, how it blinds us to the pain of those around us, bolstering us in an arrogance that keeps the untidiness and complexity of these issues out of our clean aisles of life. We shout out into the echo chamber of our social groups, our faith communities, our neighborhoods, and reassurance is boomeranged back to us that, yes, we've done all we can, and no, it's not all that bad, and, yes, if someone really wants to change their opportunities, their open doors, their hopes, well then, it's just a simple matter of putting their minds to it. It doesn't mean you should be inconvenienced, or I should be inconvenienced, or we should actually work toward and embrace change.

The shadowlands. That's where we keep shoving these intrinsic issues. And then we're surprised when a spotlight sweeps over the landscape and shows us again that there are those living eclipsed, apart from the promise of this country and of what should be the inclusive ethics of its people of faith.

Since I've been back home, that experience at the Newark terminal has occurred to me over and again. And I've found myself looking for more . . . more variety in the company I keep and more ways to consider things. And I've been reminded that right here in this quaint small town of mine, there's so much richness in diversity. For certain, it might not seem as obvious at first glance, but I find it when I look a little closer.

One to another, I would just encourage you and I both to take the time to expand our gaze into the eyes of our neighbor. Ask them about their days and their ways. Let's let that exposure be the gem it is, an opportunity to engage with someone's story. Even more, let's resist the nudge to convince them that our story is better. While we might notice the divergence in our journey and theirs, let's also listen for the intersections of universal similarity. A wonder about the meaning of life. A hope for love. A desire to belong. And outside of the great big questions, just what we should make for dinner or do on the weekend. You see, so many things connect us. In today's polarized political economy and agenda-driven climate, we often trade the exploration of another's perspectives for the insistence of our own. It couldn't hurt us to pause to consider the collective core of humanity. To trust that, most likely, we are all really doing the very best we can to navigate through life and work and love and family and all the things. We all are. All of US.

LIMELIGHT

My husband garners attention nearly everywhere we go. He's known for his style and swagger. His nickname in college was

"Hollywood." When we were dating, a guy asked my friend, "Is Ben from Europe? He just seems so cool and different."

I cracked up.

Europe? Please. Waddy is the answer. He's from a place in Kentucky called Waddy, where the town landmark is an actual dump.

But you know, he's always had a "thing" about him. People just notice him.

For example, one time we were headed down an escalator and heard, "Oh my GAW! That guy is famous!" Ascending to my right was a crew of high school boys pointing at Ben. They started to walk down the up escalator just to get a better look at him. This kind of thing happens to him with regularity. Sometimes people think he is an actor. Sometimes they tag him for a famous singer. And just like with the escalator boys, sometimes people think he just "looks famous," but they can't put their finger on who he is.

I once spent a night at his side when a guy in Nashville insisted that Ben was, in fact, the country music star Eric Church. This was before the dude even started downing drinks. We at first tried to dissuade him and then gave up, realizing that the more we said to the contrary, the more Joe from the bar was convinced he was talking to the famous singer. Girl, this went on for hours.

Does this happen to you? Because I don't feel like it's a thing that happens to people often. It's a thing for him. And for me to watch as it plays out while I stand next to him. Am I his manager? His handler? Maybe his wife? They may not even stop to consider me. They seem to see right past me. It doesn't really matter. They've seen him, whoever they think he is.

I approach the Starbucks counter, scanning for familiar faces to ensure my upcoming order can be executed.

Ben's drink is meticulous with menu amendments. For the first few times, when it was my turn to hit the local Starbucks on our Sunday runs, I had to consult the notes section in my phone to get it straight. Cold foam cold brew with sweet cream in it as the creamer and sweet cream foam on top. No water and no sweetener. For the love, it takes an army of Coffee Angels to whip it up.

They know him. Know the order by heart now. Smile with warmth, "Oh, Ben's drink! Yes, we know it!"

After they recall the steps of production between baristas, one looks over the counter at me, scrunches her forehead to pronounce her eleven lines, and asks, "Now what was it that you was wanting, hun?"

Just coffee. With a little heavy cream.

As if she is disappointed that my drink lacks fanfare, she repeats, "Just coffee?"

"Yes, just coffee. Heavy cream."

I take my blasé drink and wait patiently for them to pull off java magic for my husband. How can they remember all that he wants and not even register that I have never—not even once—ordered coffee any other way?

It's just coffee, right?

Actually, no.

I'm standing in the front yard of our new address in the midst of our home renovation project, visually interpreting how the living room will be decorated once we move in. My friends are standing in the yard with me, celebrating the upcoming crossing of the finish, a five-year period that has had our family bouncing all over creation, as Grandmom would say. In conversation, I trace the timeline from the first home I bought before Ben and I got married, to the one I'm standing in front of now. One of my friends pays me a kind compliment about how she loves the feel and decoration of my homes, starting with that first sweet spot on the corner of Adair Ave. The other face in our circle looks surprised at her spoken sentiment like he hadn't considered that I had some hand in anything up Ben's alley since, by trade, it's my husband who is the incredible real estate developer and designer, crazy talented in what he does. He lets this fall out of his mouth,

"Oh wow. Huh . . . I guess you're just always in your husband's shadow, Mel."

I shrink back and concede, "Yep. I guess so." My other friend's face registers understanding of what I've tried to explain to her before. It's not an impression that I have. It just is.

Here's the weird thing. Usually, when you think of living in someone's shadow, it's purely a negative thing. But what happens when you live in the shadow of someone who is your life partner and who you actually adore and admire?

Ben is a baller. He disrupts the dismal old way of doing things. He is an intrepid entrepreneur. His ideas are audacious. His imagination is inspiring. His vision is captivating. His quiet confidence paints him as intimidating for those who don't take the time to get to know him. But trust me, it's a treat to make the effort. I get it—I'm for sure biased, but I don't think I stand alone in my assessment of him.

So that's him. And I am at his side. Sometimes invisibly so.

My friend Katye wrote to me once and called me a "best-kept secret." I think of that often when people are swooning over Ben. It can be a tricky thing to navigate.

I suppose I could be bitter that he spends so much time in the limelight. And there have been seasons of that.

Or I could be overly grateful that someone with such a big orbit would pair up with me. But that sentiment died off a long time ago, too. 'Cause that's a little thing known as co-dependence and trust me, your therapist isn't a big fan of that kind of dynamic.

Sometimes I do just want to be seen. You know, for me. To wave from behind him as if to say, "Hey, I'm here, too!" But time has made me wonder. Why do I need you to notice me?

Does the fact that you see me increase my value? And if you don't, does my worth decrease?

Maybe it's not that I'm eclipsed by him at all. Maybe it's not his shadow that I'm really in. Maybe it's the shadow of self-doubt. Who am I if you don't notice me?

Who am I if you don't notice me?

And maybe THIS is one of the greatest lessons I can learn from being with him.

That my selfdom can exist inside or outside or beside his world and you can think what you will of it either way or not at all, and I'm just fine. I'm so much better than just fine.

This has been gold I've had to mine for, but what a treasure it is.

I've come to really know who I am and to love the me that goes unnoticed as I stand beside him while people ask for "his" autograph. To be content as I repeat my boring coffee order for the eighty-seventh time while they whip up his complex caffeine request. To let him shine in the lane he's paved and to go about my way on my own less prominent path.

And you know what's even better than the lessons in self-assurance? The desire to notice others unseen and to be a spotlight that shines on them. To see the one to the left or the right of center stage and to say, "Tell me more about you." To encourage those who've been pushed in the corners or who just happen to find themselves there for whatever reason. To step into their shadow, place my hand on their shoulder, and walk them into their own shine.

Eclipsed by Addiction

A ddiction is sneaky. At first, it's like swimming; the water feels great, and you're floating and light. After a while, you start to get tired, and you want to get out of the water, but you can't. Your limbs get heavy, and everything is weighty and dark, and it's not swimming anymore. It's more like drowning because something is pressing your head deep down under the water. And you almost just let it kill you. But if you can find your way back up to the surface and out of it, and you take great big life-giving breaths, you won't want to let it take you down again.

Just before I sank all the way under, a helping hand reached out for me. It had extended love many times before as I continued to dip into the depths, but this time I met the grip of grace and held on tight.

I'm breathing deeply now, but I will use these pages to tell you about the addiction that nearly eclipsed a life fully lived and to celebrate the exhilarating inhales and releasing exhales this new air is providing me.

HOW IT HAPPENED

You know those cute little signs that all the really good moms make for their kids to hold up on the first day of school? They have the child's name and grade on them. Some moms stop there. Others have a slew of prompts about their kids' favorite foods, their favorite colors, what they love, who their hero is, what they want to be when they grow up, and more. You can see the sea of signs on social media on "First Day of School" updates that flood feeds across the world everywhere in early fall. Based on the future resumes listed on these First Day of School signs, I'm amazed at how many kids imagine themselves as teachers, doctors, and veterinarians. Not many professional projections for undertakers or paralegals. Just sayin'.

You know what else I never see written as something someone wants to be when they grow up?

An addict.

And why?

Because no one dreams of one day suffocating.

No one imagines they'll chart a course for themselves that will lead to suffering.

I haven't heard of a case in which someone willfully decides to trade a life of freedom for a life of bondage to the bottle. (Or syringe or pantry or prescription or . . .) You get me.

As a child or even as a young adult, I never could have supposed that I'd be writing these words on this side of sobriety because I could not begin to conceptualize that I would ever come so close to losing my life to the hellscape of addiction.

But I did.

I've tried on lots of hats for jobs and sometimes have more than one at once. My chalkboard sign would have read: I Want to Be a Teacher, but I grew up to be a lot of things. Sales Rep.

Pilates Instructor. Doula. Restaurateur. Entrepreneur. Freelance Writer. Wellness Director. Realtor. And, alas, Addict.

No one saw it coming.

I was the president of the Drug Free Club in high school. I drank a little in college at frat parties and on spring break but didn't like the way alcohol made me feel. I had an occasional sugary spirit here and there after graduation but was always careful just to enjoy one or two drinks.

At my first training for my pharmaceutical job, a girl beside me ordered a glass of chardonnay. The demands and rigor of our training were super stressful, and she suggested that a few sips would take the edge off.

A few sips turned into gulps, and I was soon ordering wine every night with dinner during the week.

Then there was a night of several rum and diet cokes and a karaoke bar and a next day head-pounding hangover. But I still drank the following night again. I was just trying to make the best of my training and to network with my new colleagues, after all.

When the ten-week training was over and I was back home, I told myself I would reset. This is just life at training.

But the cravings were strong.

Once I got back to my regular life, I kept the cravings at bay and stayed mostly dry during the weeks. But I was now drinking on the weekends.

I moved next to neighbors who invited us over nearly every night for cocktails. Midori daiquiris. Invitation accepted.

When I started dating Ben, I thought my new life would mean less reason to numb out. I was right. When I was with him, we drank on occasion but nothing regular.

Except margaritas once or twice during the week.

Then I met and fell madly in love with Merlot. I found myself buying a bottle each time I made a grocery run. Then I started running to the grocery more often.

Soon I started grabbing a couple of bottles to keep from having to run out for more midweek.

Ben didn't care much for wine, which meant I was polishing those bottles off on my own. *Just because I'm an enthusiast doesn't mean I'm a disciple*, I told myself.

I tried to taper down and have just one glass a day. I bought a bigger glass. Like, the biggest goblet available at TJ Maxx.

I justified two glasses based on some study I read about high blood pressure and red wine.

I started having to lie to myself regularly about my "could-be" problem during nightly negotiations about whether I should slow down.

I was up to two servings in what were basically bowls on a sturdy stem, and that equaled nearly a whole bottle. *Everyone knows red wine turns to vinegar if you don't drink it pretty soon, and also, there's the whole waste factor, so I might as well finish that little bit that's left to keep from having spoiled wine in the morning.*

I made it through two pregnancies without drinking, *so obviously I'm not an alcoholic.* I mean, I did have an occasional sip of merlot when I was able to balance the glass on my belly. I told myself it was a very European thing to do.

Once the babies were earthside, bring mama a drink. And another one.

Then I was drinking as soon as I started dinner each night.

I remember Ben gently nudging once, "I see you're having a lot of wine lately. Are you okay?" I laughingly said, "I know. I think I'm just . . . I dunno. Do you think maybe I have a drinking problem?" Somehow that conversation ended with us gig-gling. Was it too much for him to consider? Was it too much for me to imagine? *Ha ha, isn't that silly? To think I'd have a drinking problem?*

I looked at our recycling bin at the end of the week, and there it was—a collection of seven wine bottles. That no one else had touched but me. *Oh shit.*

I started doing quarterly cleanses. I'd eat from a list of approved foods and not drink. I felt incredible. And as soon as that time was up, I'd keep with the healthy eating habits I'd formed but ease my way back to the bottle. Eventually, the cleanses were just from food, and I counted wine as an approved fruit.

I experienced heartbreak, the kind that can completely shatter you. I didn't want to feel the pain, so I tried my best not to. And vodka numbed faster than wine. *Plus, it's inconspic-uous. You can't really smell it, and it looks like water.*

Around this time, I couldn't escape that what started as an emotional connection to alcohol had been eclipsed by a physical dependence on it. The weekend ritual became the one-glass-a-night routine, which grew into the daily habit that had undoubtedly become an addiction.

And then we opened a bar.

I've always been one for efficiency.

So, no more runs to CVS if I was out of anything. Just go "check on things at the bar," and oh wow, look what fell into my twenty-ounce to-go coffee cup—vodka!

Now I was acting like an addict:

Putting bottles in different trash cans around our properties.

Canceling workout classes I was teaching because I couldn't pull it together at 5:15 a.m. enough to do burpees.

Tucking cash away on vacation so I could buy a drink or two at the bar "under the radar" and drink it while I waited for my other one to be made, the one I'd charge to the room— the only one accounted for.

Making next-day phone calls to people to apologize for what I said the night before, most of which I remembered, and *I'm sorry.*

Picking fights with Ben over stuff sober Mel didn't have the courage to discuss and that drinking Mel didn't have the wherewithal to discuss with sense.

Forgetting something each one of my girls said happened. By forgot, I mean blacked out. By blacked out, I mean I had an alcohol-induced blackout and missed an entire thing with my girls.

I was drinking not because I wanted to. I was drinking because I needed to.

I drank for the diary dumper. For the girl whose heart was overlooked by the one she gave to hold it. I drank for the girl who tried to keep everyone happy. The girl who was told she wasn't enough. I drank for the girl who swallowed the truth to keep the peace. I drank for the girl who gave most of her waking hours to a job that left her empty. The girl who kept repositioning herself in the pews that had stopped being comfortable a long time ago. The girl who succeeded at things that didn't

I drank because I was grieving the girl I thought I'd be.

much matter to her, and the one who didn't realize success in what did matter to her. The girl who longed for roots.

Really, most overwhelmingly, I drank because I was grieving the girl I thought I'd be.

And then, one day, an alarm sounded in my soul system:

There's still time to be that girl.
Or anyone you want to be, really.

But you have to be all-in to be her.
You were made for more than this mess you've created.

I had to let my addiction die in order to resurrect my life. And so began the way back to myself.

But I'm living now.

All in.

One day at a time.

THE HARDEST THING

The hardest thing about waking up is piecing together the puzzle of last night.

Did I do all the mom things? Pack lunches, sweet tuck-ins, sign permission slips. Check.

Did I respond to that email (and was it reasonable)? (Quick outbox scan . . .) Check.

Did I pick a fight with Ben and, if so, did I smooth it over enough before passing out, or are we working it out this morning? Foggy replay. Shew. Agreeable evening? Check.

And for God's sake, did I tuck the bottle of Tito's into the cereal box in the recycling bin or leave it out? (Scurry to bin . . .) Thanks to muscle memory, Check.

Exhale. (But not one of those deep healing breaths. Just a short, strained release of my routine early morning scan ticking off well.)

Now, strong coffee, B vitamin load, and a bit of peppermint oil, and I should be good to go.

No one's up yet, so by the time they roll out of bed, the swelling in my face should be mostly gone. If not, I can go with the allergy bit. Springtime in Kentucky offers that as a consistent storyline. Great. That's covered.

I think that's everything.

Mkay, this is a lot.

I wonder what morning would look like if this wasn't the way.

This is the last morning I'm doing this. I'm never drinking again. I mean, it'll be hard for a few nights just because it's a great way to cap off the day, but I'm good. This is not a problem. So, this'll be fine. I'll be fine. It'll all be fine.

Oh wait—I can't quit today. La Cocina with the girls tonight. So, margaritas tonight, quitting tomorrow. Ugh! We've got the farm-to-table dinner Saturday and Ciarra makes the best gin and tonics with the grapefruit and mint. And Sunday is sangria day. Sangria Sunday! Okay. So, Monday. And since I'm quitting Monday, I might as well go all-in until then. I'll see if anyone wants to meet for a drink before dinner.

JESUS AND LARRY

I have to get out of here. My ears are ringing. Every sound seems louder. Intensified. Amplified. But none of them can drown out the cry of my addiction urging me, "Driiiiiiiink!!"

In desperation for distraction, I grab my keys and tell Ben I am going for a drive. Nothing he can do or say tonight will be right, and that doesn't mean he'll be doing anything wrong. It's better if I just go out for a bit.

I need a pack of batteries. Not for this exact moment, but it was on my list from the grocery earlier, and I forgot it, and so I will go and get it now. I just need something to do to pass the time, to distract me. I choose a stop at Walgreens instead of CVS because they do not have a liquor section. Ugh. Of course they are completely out of 9-volts. I could just go to Walmart, but against my better judgment, I drive across the street to CVS. I give myself a half-hearted, "You got this," as I pull into the parking spot.

I walk inside and scan the display shelves near the check-out counter for batteries. I know that if I have to head to the back of the store, the signal will sound. I used to love the warm invitation of the automated AI voice above me. "Welcome to our spirit shop. A member of our team will be here to help you shortly." Only a week into sobriety, she sounds like a demon in my head.

I freeze at the end of the aisle I used to so eagerly and regularly peruse. A woman from behind the counter says, "Someone will be right with you."

My immediate thought:

"Is it Jesus?!?!? Because I'm gonna need some sort of supernatural intervention here."

But my mouth doesn't say a thing. A man approaches me with a kind greeting and asks if he can be of service.

It is not Jesus.

It is just Larry.

Larry asks if I need help finding anything. I think, *"How about an AA meeting?"* but I don't want to be rude.

"I think I'm all set here. Thanks, Larry."

My feet slowly take me away from the Bulleit Bourbon that's been seducing me and propel me toward the Duracells I actually came for.

I decide to take the long way around, through the cosmetics and up to the register, so I don't have to risk the boozy landmine again. I pay for the batteries and bolt to the parking lot.

I get in the car and begin to sob. Like ugly face, snotty nose sobbing. Like shoulders shaking sobbing. Like moans of misery sobbing.

This is my life now.

It feels heavy and hard.

It takes every bit of energy I have in a day just to make it through without reaching for a drink.

And then another.

One Day at a Time seems like too much to ask.

That brief three-minute trip into a pharmacy took a day's worth of power.

I've got nothing left in me.

EVER AGAIN

The wheel steers me to my resting ground at the end of this grueling string of days. I turn into the parking lot and scan the sparkle along the water. This summer, we have been living off and on at Lake Shelby in a rented camper, just a few miles from our Main Street address. It has become my respite. The end of summer was peppered with booze blackouts, but I treasure everything I remember from this place. And it holds me like a warm hug.

I step up into the camper and open the refrigerator door for some kombucha. I gasp at what I see standing tall on the shelf. A perfectly chilled bottle of Josh Cellars chardonnay. I hadn't been back since I stopped drinking a week ago.

I imagine the crisp kiss of the first sip and begin negotiations.

No one is here.

No one would know.

Quitting cold turkey may be too big of a step.

What if you just tapered down?

Maybe January would be a good time to stop.

Who stops when it still feels like summer out? Is now really the best time?

I have argued those same points and many others time and time again. I know I'm bullshitting myself.

I reach for the wine, twist open the top, and dart out of the camper door. I turn the bottle upside down and pour out what has become poison to me. The only thing falling faster than the wine are the tears rushing from my eyes.

I throw the empty bottle away and start to pace. Scurry really. Back and forth between the dam and the camper, trying to walk off the want for the wine. My chest is tight and stingy. I move for a while until I can collect myself enough to start to come back to my breath.

Inhale to the count of five, hold for the count of five, exhale to the count of five.

As my breath slows, so does my racing heart.

I head back inside the camper and collapse into the cushion on the bench seat. I'm totally drained. I start to close my eyes, but before I can, quite a strange thing happens.

I feel a darkness sliver into the room and settle over the atmosphere.

It's a real thing.

A visible shadow.

A presence I could almost touch if I wanted to.

But I didn't.

It's hard to explain except by saying this, so I will. I don't know how else to describe it.

It was like a physical manifestation of my addiction.

Or maybe it wasn't "like" anything.

Maybe it just was.
I rub my eyes and refocus.
Still there.
I hinge forward and place my forearms on top of my legs
and clasp my hands.
I look right at it.
I don't shift my gaze for a second.
It's a face-off between us.
It may last a few minutes or an hour. I'm not sure,
but I am unwavering in my resolve.
This thing has come to swallow me up.
Somehow I stare it down with a strength that isn't mine.
And then I speak to it.
"Listen, I don't exactly understand this or you, but I do
know you're real.
And I know you're here for me.
But here's the thing.
You can't have me.
Ever again."
And then I am quiet.
I have said all there is to say.
Now I just have to wait for it to leave.
So I wait.
And so it leaves.

NO FINISH LINE

I am approaching the One Year sobriety mark.

I am at dinner with my tribe of girlfriends. We're all catching up on kid stuff and summer recaps and job updates,

everything we've missed since the last dinner, and details that can't fit on our text string.

One of the girls enthusiastically says, "Mel, tell us about how you're feeling with your One Year coming up?" She beams with pride for me, and the others break out in encouragement.

And I break out in tears.

Such a strange response.

Completely unexpected.

"Ummm . . . well, I mean . . . I'm excited. I guess. I mean . . . it's a big deal for sure, and I've fought my ass off to get here. But it feels weird too."

These are the friends who got daily and then weekly counts of my days of sobriety. They texted and called with virtual love when I hit mile markers. One month. Three months. Six months. And now, this upcoming One Year mark.

I suppose it's not until this moment that I realized there is no actual finish line to this race.

Just more mile markers.

It's not like you can ever outrun your addiction. It's always there. But you can outpace it. And it does get easier.

It's not like an actual marathon where you condition and train and run and then rest. There is no resolve. With addiction, you just keep conditioning and training, and running. And there is no rest. And the weight of that daunting truth presses down on me so heavily that I can barely speak.

It's not like you can ever outrun your addiction. It's always there.

But you can outpace it.

And it does get easier.

And at some point, along this route of redemption, I

stopped racing away from the ghosts of addiction and just kept running onward, toward a life fully lived.

TWO YEARS SOBER

At the end of my yoga practice, I can hear my teacher say in a low, calm voice, "Slowly begin to bring your awareness back to your breath. Deepen your breath. Wiggle your fingers and toes to bring movement back into your body . . . " and on she goes to invite us to come back into the day.

That's how it felt . . . coming back into my body and reconnecting with my spirit through sobriety. At the beginning, it was absolute hell. The promise of making it to the other side of my daily pours seemed weak compared to the immediate angst that was my constant companion. It was such labor to pace my breath as I was riddled with anxiety. But over days that turned into weeks that turned into months, I began to not only bring awareness back to my breath but to breathe deeply again. Instead of frantic rapid-fire sips of air, I came to lengthen my breaths and steady my soul.

Bringing movement back into my body was first a problem and then a process. At first, checking in with my body was like reminding myself how much I wanted alcohol. My body was yelling at me to give it something that would kill it. I was in literal pain from letting go of what I had white-knuckled for so long. Feeling my body's messages, the ones I had been numbing until I could feel them no more . . . well, it was horrific. There were days I wanted to peel my skin off to escape the throes of withdrawals. I had to relearn wellness, even though I had taught it for years. I had to completely reset with rest, prayer, and self-care like meditation, yoga, trail runs, therapy, writing, tea, or baths . . . anything that brought me wholeness. Every day. Every day it got a little easier. And now I'd n e v e r want to go back to that bondage.

And so today marks two years of being sober. Seven hundred and thirty days of rebirth. Of waking. Of emerging. Of living. Of bringing my awareness back to my breath.

Inhaling peace, exhaling chaos.
Inhaling truth, exhaling lies.
Inhaling hope, exhaling shame.
Inhaling light, exhaling shadows.
Inhaling life, exhaling death.

A TOAST TO THE ORDINARY

The rhythm of rain and Patty Griffin are the background to this Tuesday evening in my kitchen. The girls are folding laundry in the guest room, and Ben hasn't made it home from his rounds at all his projects yet. I pour a concoction of cranberry and ginger kombucha into a white wine glass and silently celebrate that it's been three and a half years since my last vodka tonic.

I chop onions, cube sweet potatoes, cut broccoli, and line them in the pan categorically, like the Neapolitan variety of to-be roasted vegetables. I drizzle them with avocado oil, salt, and pepper, set an entire topless bulb of garlic in a corner by the purple onion, and slide the baking sheet into the oven. I draw my attention next to de-stemming and massaging the large leathery leaves of kale with a pinch of sea salt to soften and darken the bitter bites, making them more pleasing to the palate. While the vegetables are roasting, I gather ingredients for the dressing—a simple combination of balsamic vinegar, olive oil, and coarse sea salt, and let it sit in the Vitamix as I wait for the roasted garlic to be done. I toast slivered almonds and set them to cool.

While dinner cooks, it's just me and the music from the speakers and the sky. And then I add my own with an enthusiastic take at the chorus my heart knows so well, both from repetition and understanding:

> "But if you break down
> I'll drive out and find you
> If you forget my love
> I'll try to remind you
> And stay by you when it don't come easy."[6]

The smell of lemony dill and the timer tell me that the salmon is ready. I draw it out of the oven and set it to rest on the stovetop. I pull out the now-browned rows of roots and cruciferous mix and add them to the bowl of prepped kale. I plop a few bulbs of garlic into my dressing mixture—and then one more for good measure since it's flu season. I blend the ingredients into a creamy sauce and drizzle it over the warm salad. Salivating. This is one of my favorite meals. I sprinkle the toasted almonds over the dish and plate it, and pair it with the salmon. Almost ready!

I call for the girls when I hear the climb of Ben's footsteps up to the loft. My heart is full. He slides his arms around my waist as I'm rinsing a dish in the sink, and we sway side to side for a few notes. Having heard their daddy, Cel and Annie come darting down the hall to attack him with love. Annie insists, "Group hug," and we all squeeze in together. We collectively grab napkins and drinks and line the kitchen island for dinner. Recounts of daily happenings and girly giggles drown out Patty and any other care in the world that I might have.

I lift my spiritless glass, turn the stem between my fingers, take a lingering sip, and mentally toast that I am fully here for this completely ordinary moment.

Cheers. Cheers to the magnificent ordinary.

Eclipsed by Routine

Sometimes routine is the only way to survive. When something unforeseen rains down, the rituals and schedules and daily obligations are the shelter that keeps us moving forward.

And sometimes routine turns to sleepwalking. We stumble from day to day, rinse, repeat, letting the current of what must be done carry us, instead of letting each day have its own light. Sleepwalking born of routine keeps us half asleep, restless but not moving forward, responding to shadow dreams instead of our real, waking life.

TIDAL LOCKING

It gives me pause every time the moon shows itself in the night sky. She never ceases to captivate my attention. As a girl, I imagined that there really was a man in the moon. Way back when, I wondered if that might be where God lived. I dreamed of Him working hard all day—going and going and going to take care of everything and everyone He made. Because He needed to rest after so much work, I pictured the moon as

His heavenly bedroom where He'd rest at night after He put away the sun. In my mind, Heaven was just behind the veil of the sky, but God wanted us to see his silhouette so we would know He was looking over us.

As I got older, church taught me that God lived in Heaven and science taught me that the moon was no place you'd want to live, so I put away that childish idea. Still, it was a sweet sentiment for my little girl self to be endeared to for a time. Regardless, the sight of the sky's night light still takes my breath away. I'm especially impressed by the fact that it looks like it's up there doing its own thing, charting its own course.

In reality, it's locked to the Earth's orbit. It's a phenomenon called Tidal locking. It happens when an orbiting astronomical body always has the same face toward the object it is orbiting. This is known as synchronous rotation: the tidally locked body takes just as long to rotate around its own axis as it does to revolve around its partner.

Sometimes I feel like the moon. I'm in constant motion, and it looks like I'm making progress. But sometimes, when I lean in a bit to take a closer look, I can see it: I'm not really moving on my own. As women, I think it's something we might all take a closer look at. Are we in motion because we are in the business of charting our own course, or are we just following a bigger personality, an influencer, a faith teacher, a parent, a partner, a friend, our kids?

Are we in motion because we are in the business of charting our own course, or are we just following a bigger personality, an influencer, a faith teacher, a parent, a partner, a friend, our kids?

Have we attached ourselves to someone else's orbit for a sense of power? Maybe we don't even realize it, this attachment. Maybe it's out of a compulsion to people please. Maybe it's because we have been following the same pattern for so long—in life, in love, in response—that we've stopped asking why we're doing things the way we are. We've been outside our own course for so long that we don't even know how we got here or how to find our way back.

Take parenting, for example. Our trajectory runs parallel to our children's for many years. It's the nature of nurturing our families.

In marriage, parenting, and partnerships, it's natural and beautiful for our paths to intertwine. The trouble comes when one person is so tethered to the sway of another that she's forgotten her way. It usually starts off slowly. You find interest in or glean meaning from someone. They simply hold your regard at first. Over time, this force begins to have more weight in our worlds. When someone's gravitational pull is stronger than ours, we can be sucked into their orbit. We're spinning, but we've merged out of our own story because we're keeping in step with theirs. It's motion, but it's not organically ours.

Maybe that cute guy full of charisma got your number and then your interest, and then your spotlight. He's larger than life, and so you shrink back to make more space for him.

Maybe it's the continuing influence of your parents in your life. Their pull keeps you spinning about what they will think and what they might disapprove of in your life, and what they might give you kudos for. You're tidal locked on that relationship, always keeping the face you think they want to see toward them, constantly tracking their responses.

Perhaps you're restricted in your own path because you're so closely adhering to the social norms of your community or faith circle.

Some of us find ourselves under the spell of social influencers, and we scour their feeds to tell us how to decorate, dress, eat, invest, and even believe.

We forfeit our individuality to follow someone else, and so there's a loss of our own significance. Pretty soon, if we're not careful, we can forget how to think for ourselves and, eventually, how to even be ourselves.

We tend to orbit others' lives, so we forget or never realize that we too have Light.

While overcoming being tidal locked to someone can be layered and complex, the first step isn't really. The first step is just a question. And that question is this:

Why am I doing the things I'm doing?

Why do you feel guilty when you don't want to volunteer to work the baked goods booth at the school fundraiser? If the answer is that you don't want to ignite the ire of the PTA, you might be tidal locked.

Why do you think you can't paint your bedroom a color that you love but every decor influencer on social media says that it's not trendy? Tidal locked.

Why are you making most of your moments about your partner's schedule, your kids' routines, and your extended family's calendar while pushing down feelings of overwhelm and fatigue and needing a reset? Might be a raging case of tidal locking.

> **We forfeit our individuality to follow someone else, and so there's a loss of our own significance. Pretty soon, if we're not careful, we can forget how to think for ourselves and, eventually, how to even be ourselves.**

Breaking from being tidal locked isn't a license to live only according to what only we want, need, and like. All healthy relationships have seasons where flexibility and focus move from one person to the next, a gentle dance that can breathe and improv and adjust to what's going on in life. Overcoming chronic tidal locking isn't achieved by commanding others to be tidal locked to us. It's about maintaining a balance where the people we love and our souls find the ability to soar, to be seen, to be safe, depending on what the season brings.

CRESCENDO

The chorus crescendos as the drumbeat drives the rhythm into full throttle. Every hand around me is raised, and some people are so overcome that they are weeping. Claps and cheers are heard throughout the congregation, with enthusiastic calls of "Yessss!" My heart pounds with the pulse of the music. A few folks have stepped out into the aisle and are physically bowing down at this point. One woman circles the church with a banner that reads "Holy Holy Holy." It seems like our worship has opened a portal to heaven and like God just may actually be inhabiting the praises of His people, as it is written. A man blows the shofar from his usual position at the back left corner of the sanctuary, and the crowd goes wild. Speaking in tongues. More applause. Dancing. I'm intoxicated by it all. I hear whispers of "Hallelujah" in the row behind me as the song slows to its fade and the pastor makes his way to the stage. The band plays low behind him, layering lingering tags under his invitation for us to search our hearts. He encourages us to renew our relationship with Jesus today or to ask him to be the Lord of our lives if we have never known him as our Savior. A few hands go up, signaling their response to the altar call. Some people migrate to the front. Some are so overcome by the Spirit of God that they fall under His power. Like a Holy Ghost hypnosis.

Eventually, we all migrate out of the church over the course of several moments. I'm buzzed and heightened but also wiped out. Like I've just run a marathon. And I likely could have in the hours we've been here.

It can be a hard plummet from the high-velocity place I've just left. Most of us can't remain in that intense engagement. After all, at some point, you've got to leave. What's more, you've got to do normal things like fold laundry and go to the grocery and feed your dog. And so, you can't stay at that peak. When you leave that kind of atmosphere, you're literally disconnected from the experience, the source that's been feeding your emotions. Then, we are sometimes left to wonder if we're detached from the actual Source behind it all.

The spiritual mountaintop experience is spellbinding. Some of us peak at revivals, worship conferences, even church camp. Some of us have weekly church services that offer up such fervor. Typically, the set and setting have been carefully designed with us in mind. It's easy to be swept up in the strategic sentimental soundbites and moved by the masterminded catalysts meant to spur us on. Production is pervasive in our culture-bound religion, catering to our preferences based on market-based research of our prototype. There's a whole psychology behind an event, like the Wizard of Oz winding the crank behind the curtain to ensure that there's a regular rise of emotions, a nice stay near the top, the actual peak, and then the 'send you on your way' song. It's easy to miss the warning signs of how manipulative the whole thing can be.

I'm not even saying these things are necessarily bad. Maybe it's not. After all, it's how we formulate school programs, business strategies, and marketing campaigns. The trouble is when we become reliant on it, when we confuse it for burning bush levels of connection to God.

I mean, let's be honest. The system has created what we've asked for. We, the consumers, want the entertainment value of it all. We climb that momentary ascent, and then our buzz dissipates.

And what if we go and then we don't get the hit? Maybe we arrive at the gathering late. (Because now Sunday services are often trendily called "gatherings" or "celebrations," catering to those of us who might struggle with traditions of our past or the idea of a service performed by rote.) Maybe we didn't like the songs. Maybe the sermon was boring. Maybe we're disappointed. If we're not captured by the message or the music, we're likely moving on down the road to the next show, to see if the crank behind their curtain is turning out what we like. We're making lots of spiritual choices today based on stagecraft and strategy.

Maybe I grew so reliant upon the production of 'church' on stage to feed my spirit. To be clear, God did not prescribe any of this. It was me who was reliant upon the production of church to open up a portal to heaven for me. And when that didn't work for me anymore, I wondered how I could access heaven at all.

I have a long history of high-octane spiritual experiences, but I've also made other stops on the protestant tour, from Presbyterian to Methodist to Southern Baptist. No banners. No shofar. No fireworks.

Eventually, I found myself as part of a church worship team. In that role, I felt responsible for creating that high I'd gone in pursuit of for so many years. We never quite made it to what I'd call the mountaintop in that rented school cafeteria that housed our church services, but we topped a few hills.

I realized along the way that people, me included, were showing up to church to "get God," like God was a loaf of bread. God is not a commodity just because we've commercialized Him. We go scavenging for external spiritual cues and assurances of what? That God thinks we're enough? That God sees us? What are we searching for in those external versions of worship? It's taken me some time to realize that you can't get more of what's already inside of you.

> **God is not a commodity just because we've commercialized Him.**

After a while, it became more and more difficult for me to have a pure church experience without overthinking the production and predictability of it all. And even still, I sometimes wished I could *unrealize* what had become so apparent.

I suppose the silver lining is that I stopped going to church with an agenda to get God. But eventually, I just stopped going to church altogether. When I stepped outside of our Sunday morning routine and began exploring God outside the walls, I just wanted to press the mute button on the dominant narrative and sit quietly. I say this gently, but for me . . . I felt like I just needed to detox from church. I had this sense that I'd been in a religion-induced trance for long enough. I needed the quiet to settle my spirit.

When I leaned into contemplative practices, it was curious to me that those customs were so meaningful and yet not attached to emotionalism at all. There seemed to be no rise in the tide. Just a slow and steady stream, a flow. When we are removed or remove ourselves from a thing long enough to look at it from a new viewpoint, we might be surprised at our original perspective. As I glance back at the places I've come from, it seems I didn't realize until I was outside of it how kind of odd it all was.

My reflections on it all are a bit jarring. I see now how much I relied on it. And that's where the danger is. There were seasons where I relied on an emotion-leveraging, razzle-dazzle church experience on Sunday mornings as much as I did on vodka on Sunday evenings.

The problem is not the stage or even that crank turner behind the curtain. The trouble comes when the experience we show up looking for eclipses the real Source that the experience is supposed to be spotlighting.

I'm here to tell you, it's a big shift from Bethel to Merton. From Hillsong to a quiet hillside. From the shofar to silent meditation.

I miss those mountaintop experiences sometimes. It has been interesting to learn how to worship without the consistent impetus evoking my emotions, moving me from glory to glory.

Some of us have been herded through or have willfully chosen a Jesus genre that is more hushed and collected in its posture toward God. Others spend Sundays doing the Holy Ghost Hop.

Who's to say what's more real? Not me.

My guess is that both belong.

And because God is everywhere, it stands to reason that God is there, in both the crescendo and the quiet.

CAR FIX

Ben and I have pulled off a parenting surprise that will blow their little minds! We've planned a trip to Disney, and they have not one single clue. I've written a note "from their favorite Disney characters" who tell them about the trip. We will put it just outside their door for them to see in the morning. But for now, it's time to tuck in for the night.

Both girls are snuggled in under the blankets and we're recapping their day. Annie is sucking her thumb and holding her lovey "Maggie" close to her face, stroking the soft material across her cheek. Annie is as sweet as a ripe peach, whereas her lovey is rancid from being dragged all over everywhere she goes, but the two still make a cute pair. Celia's strawberry blonde curls are fanned out over the pillowcase and she's holding both of my hands in hers. Her sleepy scratchy voice asks, as if on cue, "What are we doing tomorrow?"

I don't own a poker face, so this is a difficult moment for me. I am outlining a fabricated schedule for the upcoming day with my words but am wondering if my face reads *Mickey Mouse*. I note that we need to get up early tomorrow to help take Mimi, our name for my mom, to get her car fixed. Celia asks seven questions about said needed trip to the mechanic to make sure she knows exactly what's going down at Doug's Tire with Mimi's Toyota. Obviously by her line of questioning these are things that are imperative for her to understand because she likes to make sure she has a full scope of knowledge in order to know what to anticipate. For the love, I have now explained tire rotation, oil changes, and something about gauges that I completely devise on the spot. It's now past their normal bedtime and my patience clock is punched. I offer up a quick prayer over them, load them up with kisses all over their freckles, and assert, "Don't let your feet hit the floor when I leave. It's time for sweet sleep, my loves. See you when the sun comes up." (Read: *I'm not far behind you on bedtime myself and this princess letter is about to be delivered and I don't want you to see it 'til morning so do.not.even. think.about.getting.out.of.that.bed.*)

Thankfully, their little feet do stay under the sheets all night. Ben and I smile at each other the next morning when we hear them stirring in the next room. We listen as they walk to their door to open it, finding the magical memo about our upcoming trip.

Celia curiously calls for us to come and see what they've found. Annie's eyes are wide but sleepy and she smiles at us with her thumb still in her mouth, her pointer finger hooked over her nose and Maggie in her grip. Ben and I are all, "What IS it?" as we walk down the hall to them. Celia looks at the envelope on the floor at her feet, but it takes her a moment to pick it up. "It has our name on it. 'To Celia and Annie,'" she says. We all sit on their bed and the girls work together to open the envelope (which is a process that threatens the survival of the letter inside of it for sure). Gratefully, it remains intact, and the girls unfold it to read. Celia sounds out the beginning of the letter but says it's taking too long, and can I please just read it to them?

I clear my throat: "Dear Celia and Annie: We are SO excited to tell you that you are coming to see us today at DISNEY WORLD!! Pack your bags! Your flight leaves soon! We can't wait to see you!"

Annie immediately starts spinning like a top. With "Woots" at the top of her lungs, she and Maggie are jumping up and down and near crying with sheer excitement.

Celia is composed. Almost stoic. Is she in so much shock that she can't freak out? What is happening? Ben and I are trying to infuse her with our excitement. She smiles but her face is full of questions. And then, "But Mama. I thought you said we were helping Mimi get her car fixed. Who is gonna take her now?"

And there it was. This kid who thrives on knowing with exactness what will happen next was completely thrown off by our ruse. It's like she had to reroute her entire brain to plan a new day after she had counted on the fabricated schedule we mapped out for her the night before.

Ben and I had exactly one second to pivot from what we had also planned on, absolute elation from both girls, to attend to Celia's hesitancy. We didn't have anything in the arsenal for this kind of response. Once we assured Celia that we cooked up our agenda so that she would be surprised and that Big Dad (my dad's grandfather name) had in fact planned to take Mimi to get her car fixed all along, then she was able to release herself from what she had originally banked on.

My face was begging her to get hyped with us.

"DISNEY!! We are not going to Doug's. We are going to DIIIIIIISSNEY!!! As in, THE MAGIC KINGDOM!! Isn't that AMAZING?!?!?!"

Finally, after it all computed and the mental reroute was complete, she squealed, then hugged us, and joined Annie in running up and down the hall and zipping around with thrill.

But wow, it was a process getting there.

It made me wonder; how often do we miss the magic of the unexpected in our own lives by being stuck in our predictable plan? How often do we miss the sparkle of a surprise because we like the safe shade of the schedule?

When I keep step with a predetermined cadence, I feel steady on the inside. Like Celia, I like to follow the map. Early on in my addiction recovery, everyday rituals anchored me to my sobriety. I needed touch points along the way to help me work through moments of simple living that I had to learn all over again. But even long before that, I began the practice of writing out my next day before each evening's end so that I could execute my plan with efficiency. I love marking off an item on my to-do list, congratulating myself that I'm en route to a productive day. Embarrassing fact: I used to even write down my routine of meditation, exercising, and writing morning pages. There were two reasons behind this. One, I wrote them down simply for the satisfaction of having some things marked as complete before daybreak. Secondly, I loved seeing those rituals that would be waiting for me when the morning came, the sacred moments that set the tone for the flow of the following hours.

The truth is, once the girls are off to school, I launch into the unpredictable pace and pattern of the rest of the day. I lift the lid of my laptop to enter my world of writing, real estate, Airbnb management, and any number of figurative fire drills that come with tending to several businesses and buildings. My days are reactive in most ways. This has made me a strict adherent to the rituals of my only uninterrupted time and has also taught me the lessons of flexibility and quick swivels as the day spins.

Still, sometimes the unexpected jostles me, even if it's an invitation to something beautiful. Fun things that might fall into my lap can feel like impositions because it's not how I ordered things out. A spontaneous idea sounds exciting, but please give me a minute to mentally rechart my course before I give a grin with gusto. Occasionally, I'll be cranking out my day and Ben will call with an idea to spend the afternoon hanging out. I hear his enthusiasm, sit quietly, scan my neatly outlined game plan, and see that it's a choice of one or the other. A yes to his suggestion means ditching my objectives. He hears my hesitancy in the static on the other end of the phone. I remind him, "Just processing." I try to re-assign each line item to another day's window of time. He can tell that it's harder for me to get to my answer than he'd like, but we've learned each other's particularities. If I'm lucky, I let myself scrap the schedule. There are days we just can't pull it off because I am encumbered by obligations. But sometimes, the binder is the pressure I put on myself to produce and, once that sets, it's harder for me to make space within my structure. When I squirm at the suggestion of going for coffee in the middle of the morning to sit across from Ben and daydream about upcoming projects or adventures, I am reminded that I need to loosen the reins, that rhythm has become regimen.

Is it just me? Anyone else a disciple of the planner god? Anybody else white knuckle their way through the day?

When I peel back a layer of the "why," I see it now, what's behind my devotion to the to-do list. There it is, the noose of control. A sense of false security.

Looking back, I think Celia had grown to be so reliant upon exactness in some areas because the beat of our residential home life was constantly changing. She needed something to be the control with so many variables in the equation. *Me too, Cel.*

And it's also just how some of us are wired.

Still, there's magic in the serendipity of tossing the to-do list. Magic in telling my schedule that I'm the boss of it, and not the other way around. Magic in letting go sometimes, in taking the fork in the road. Sometimes it takes us, not to Doug's Tire, but all the way to the Magic Kingdom. Sometimes the best things in life are the ones we didn't see coming.

CIRCLE

Mrs. House was using games to assess what learning her students had retained over the summer break. The first-grade teacher had her class gather in the middle of the reading carpet. For reviewing shapes, Mrs. House held up a sign of a certain shape and had the students move to designated corners of the room to place their vote about which shape they thought was on the sign. Mrs. House might hold up a square and tell the kids to go to the back right corner of the room if they thought it was a circle, the back left corner of the room if they thought it was a triangle, front left corner for their square vote and front right corner if they guessed it was an oval. Then she would tell them who got the right answer. This went on for some time. After all, there are more shapes than you might think.

When she got to the hexagon, named off the options, and labeled the corners for kids to go to for their vote—hooray! All the kids got it right! They all gathered in the designated back right corner of the room, casting their hexagon vote.

That is, all the kids except for Annie.

Mrs. House prompted Annie, "Are you sure you don't think this is a hexagon?"

Annie stood confidently in the spot for her circle vote. The teacher encouraged her again, but Annie was clearly immovable. Finally, Mrs. House asked Annie to tell her what she saw.

Self-assured, Annie walked over to the picture of the hexagon that Mrs. House was holding up. She squinted her eyes to focus on the very middle of the poster. There was a tiny circle in the design where the inside angle lines met. With her finger on the circle, Annie turned to her class and said, "Right there. It's a circle. Don't you see it?"

Even with the whole class in solidarity on the popular vote, Annie chose to stand on her own. She saw what no one else did, to boot. She was not swayed by her peers to do what they did. She did not give up her focus on the circle even though the bigger picture was something else, in this case a hexagon.

This story is so telling of her personality. She's always been her own girl. And she's always seen the world a little differently. What's more, she isn't afraid of that or feel a need to hide herself when the group choice would be easier to go along with.

I may have sprinted to the hexagon corner, but not Annie. I've taught her a thing or two about self-confidence, but mostly, she's been my teacher.

It takes strong light to discern what's in the center of something. It takes a lot of trust to find the spine of your soul and stand there, straight-backed, when everyone encourages you to sway. My prayer for Annie is that she stays this true to herself. I pray that even when the world insists on its way, she can stand firm in her way. Even when the popular vote colors and shades everything. Even when she's encouraged to change her steady position. I pray she has the confidence and courage to stand, even when the crowd shifts away. That's my prayer for me, too. And that's my prayer for you.

> **It takes a lot of trust to find the spine of your soul and stand there, straight-backed, when everyone encourages you to sway.**

EVOLUTION

The frothy, foamy, fake-chemical concoction used to be the start of my every day, paired with a string of Marlboro Ultra-lights. I had an intense love for drinking gas station cappuccinos and chain-smoking cigarettes. Like a Rose and Jack kinda love. And I was going overboard. Raising the twenty-ounce Styrofoam cup to my lips was like pulling the knob back on a pinball machine, and with the first sip I could feel the sugar and caffeine start to kick in. Everything turned on and lit up as the *ting ting ting* sound sparked in my mind. "GOOOOD MORNING!!" And the Marlboros were the obvious perfect partner.

As a pharmaceutical sales rep back in those days, I'd see patients lug bags of medicines from the waiting room to the exam rooms to review and update prescriptions with their doctors. Some of them had their oxygen tanks in tow. Along the way, it began to occur to me that if I kept pounding crap coffee and nicotine into my body, I'd easily become one of those patients. And so began the slow but steady journey to a healthier version of myself.

On my way to whole living, I started subbing my Shell station coffees for a sugary Starbucks drink. Over time, I began asking for fewer pumps of hazelnut syrup at Starbucks until I was finally just having a soy latte.

Fast forward to this morning. I had a Mushroom Coffee, which is a blend of reishi, chaga, and lion's mane.

Evolution.

As far as cigarettes go, I finally quit after about forty-two failed attempts. I tried a dozen strategies, including buying cheapos that wouldn't taste as "good." (Is there really a brand that tastes *good*?) Then I tried reducing the number of cigarettes I smoked each day until I was down to just a few. But I'd always go back for them. It wasn't until I started dating Ben that I put them down forever. In short, I wanted to kiss him. A lot. And what non-smoking cutie wants to lock lips with an ashtray? I wanted better for him. And for me. So, I basically quit so we could make out. True story.

Evolution.

I started working out when I was in college. I'd hit the gym a couple of times a week but mostly just for bragging rights. *Sure, I can swing by study group after my workout.* After I realized working out helped me manage stress better, I paid more attention to how I was exercising and tried new ways of moving. Fast forward: I got certified to teach Pilates, yoga, and general fitness classes. Now I work out just about every day and absolutely love it.

Evolution.

I used to be at church three times a week as a kid. I "got saved" when I was eight. I was baptized and learned the Apostle's Creed. (Thank you for putting that to music, Rich Mullins). By all accounts, I had gotten my ticket to heaven and just needed to wait patiently to get there. No need to keep growing or asking questions or continuing to seek God.

In so many areas of our lives, we evolve. We keep going. Keep learning. Keep seeking. Keep changing. But when we do that in our faith, people get nervous. When we move out of the holding pattern between here and heaven, we start down the proverbial slippery slope. Why does the evolution of faith seem so disconcerting?

The truth is, at some point most of us question the norms of our family of origin and those practices. Though it can be scary, it's not necessarily a bad thing. It's just part of the authentication process, like the two-step verification Amazon asks for when you log into your account from a different computer. If we shift into a new perspective and then try to go back into our former ways from that different internal space, something might prompt us to really check in. Is this really me? Or is this just the system I'm used to logging into? What happens if I can't access that account anymore?

When we begin to see our traditions in a new light, some of us hunker down for shelter in our existing setting, preferring to stay sedated by the comfort of confinement. I really do understand that. It's easy to go through the motions. Some of us panic and reach for the cellophane wrap to keep everything encased. We aren't sure our religion is durable enough to withstand our expanding image of God. It's easy to stay stuck, still drinking gas station coffee and sucking down cancer sticks and holding tight to our ticket. That's why so many of us do. We stay in places where our story begins. But when what we once thought were roots become chains, it's time to reevaluate. There's a whole lot about Jesus setting us free. Free to search and try and look and ponder. He set the example for it, over and over. Turning over tables and tipping people out of their church pews.

He evolved what the establishment thought they knew about God. The God they had attempted to make safe and palatable and predictable. And I *don't* want to blunt my spiritual growth just because it's easier to stay stunted in the safety of religion.

CHURCH HISTORY

The heavy cardboard storage box was tucked away in the downstairs closet at my parents' house along with other relics from my girlhood. I lifted the top, somewhat tattered from previous visits to this portal back in time. Setting it to the side of the narrow walk-in, I lifted out the worn brown scrapbook from the early 80s and began a picture journey to my past. On one of the first construction paper pages from this particular collection was a writing prompt for a school assignment: I was to write about what I was most grateful for. In true Kentucky good girl form, I listed "God and Kentucky Fried Chicken." As an overachiever, I drew a cross and a (poor rendition of a) drumstick, extolling both King and Colonel.

Such are the loyalties of my bluegrass heart.

And while my hips and cholesterol levels mandate that I lay off my connection to the Colonel, the other entity on my grade school grateful list remains. For as long as I can remember I've always had a natural curiosity about and affinity for knowing God. I sensed God in the breeze of spring. In the smell of honeysuckles along the fence line of my Grandmom Mathis' backyard. In the early morning music my dad would sing as a wakeup alarm. I didn't have words for it yet, or know it was standard expectation for me to "have a relationship with God." I just felt both a closeness with and astonishment for something outside of me.

As a Sunday School participant in elementary grades, I learned that this "relationship" was in fact a requirement. My natural inclination was organic up until that point, but when I realized it was mandated, there formed an entangled tango between purity and performance. Before, I did not know the ins and outs of "getting saved" and didn't consider that there

Eclipsed
By Tradition

B eing from a small town in the South, I can't remem
knowing many families that didn't go to church wh
was growing up. Some of us still line the pews (or the the
seats or the folding chairs) on Sunday morning. Others o
may have spent the years after launching into our own liv
the eclipse of all the things we thought we were suppose
be and do, versus who we really are and what we actuall

Sometimes I confuse the traditions of man with the
of the Divine. But I'm learning to embrace the tension of I
by an emerging manifesto, one that continues to pic
what claims to be truth and hold it up to the Light to see i
watermarks of honesty permeate the fibers.

After all, honesty is the only thing I know that
unscramble the ambitions and control issues of humans
the goodness and love of the one I know as God.

was a prompted exchange that needed to occur for me to "get" a God I had never considered I didn't already have.

Outside of the church classroom, you might find me looking behind chairs for angels that my mom said I'd talk with from time to time. I was full of fascination for the magic of the wind and the stirring songs of the birds above me. Inside the walls of church, I found myself much more preoccupied with having exact answers. My focus shifted to getting an A in the school of religion. And I was a dedicated pupil, adhering to the carrot and stick system of salvation. Bible Trivia—where they turn the sacred scripture into a game show—was a moment to prove my commitment to Jesus. The felt board in Miss Mary's classroom was full of stick-on Ten Commandments we memorized each week, and when I read the "Thou Shalt Nots" to myself, I heard them narrated in my mind by a stern, deep-voiced, wizard-looking man who was hovering over my every move, hoping I would do the best but likely expecting me to blow it.

I mean, I get the games and gimmicks. I've now done my share of volunteering in children's church. It's not easy to wrangle wiggly kiddos into the Old Testament without some gold stars and animal crackers to strive for. It's just that the way the "strive for" mentality embedded itself into my budding heart side-tracked me from the actual resting in God. And so too in who I was in God.

Don't get me wrong—I loved church. I have such fond memories of gathering in the downstairs choir room of First Christian Church in my Cherub Choir robe busting out songs at the top of my lungs:

"I am a promise
I am a possibility

I am a promise with a capital 'P'
I am a great big bundle of potentiality

And I am learnin' to hear God's voice
And I am tryin' to make the right choice
I am a promise to be anything God wants me to be."[7]

I loved Sunday mornings when I would go with my daddy to the nursing homes in town to serve communion and sing for the sweet smiles staring back at me. I was a junior deaconess and acolyte and played in the bell choir. Wednesday nights meant fellowship hall dinners with cousins and neighbors and friends, along with warm dinner rolls and lukewarm everything else. I was mesmerized by my mom's voice during contattas. I learned to sing harmony each week sitting between my Grandmom and my Aunt Lea, the scratchy soprano of the former and the rich alto of the latter. Their voices would rise and fall and swirl through the lyrics of "In the Garden." It was a treasured time.

It's just that I lost some of my wonder along the way and traded it in for a performance mindset. Even still, in the midst of reciting the script, I always found myself peering behind the curtain to see what might really be going on off set. I had a subtle sounding alarm that signaled me to be careful, to not be fully indoctrinated by the program. The lines continued to blur. The pursuit being described to me from the pulpit to the potlucks seemed to be less focused on knowing God and more focused on knowing *about* God. I learned the answers to the questions that I was supposed to regurgitate, but that didn't stop me from having my own examinations.

It's one reason I was so crazy about my youth pastor, Sally. Pastor Sally gave us plenty of elbow room for exploration. She encouraged our inquisitiveness and made space for our formative minds to . . . well, form. In fact, she was the one who re-awakened my curiosity by taking us on my first of many trips to the Abbey of Gethsemani.

But the wind shifted. It was my freshman year when Sally left the church. I missed her terribly. I was a blossoming flower whose roots lacked water and whose petals wilted a bit when she left. I still loved my home church but now it was mostly because my Grandmom was there. I revered her almost as much as Jesus. Some families had left as leadership changed hands, and it was definitely not the church of my earlier years. It was easy to accept an invitation to tag along to a friend's youth group one week at the local Presbyterian church. Quite simply, this was the most fun bunch of kids I had ever been around. We put on plays and organized dinners and went on road trips and enjoyed equal parts spiritual growth and teenage shenanigans. And I felt like I belonged with them.

Around the same time I found that sweet spot, my parents started to attend a full gospel charismatic church. If you aren't familiar with that brand of faith community, it's all things expressive and emotional, expectant that God will show up, literally, to do miraculous things. Particularly if you know just the right way to pray and just the right things to say. The way I remember the move to a charismatic church is that my mom visited the pastor of that church for some guidance on how to seek God in a way that yielded desired results. My parents visited one Sunday after her meeting and essentially never went back to the church of my childhood. They would go to the charismatic church on Sunday mornings and I would land at the Presbyterian church. Truth be told, some Sundays I skipped church altogether, so clearly, I had learned to bend the rules a bit by then.

The summer before my junior year in high school I went to a church camp in Montreat, North Carolina. If you weren't raised going to church camp, it's a rite of passage for a lot of church kids. It's a week of every kind of ice breaker, group chat, worship gatherings designed to inspire guilt and tears, and a varsity level of flirtation and romance that is wildly ignited by the close-knit quarters of raging hormones and continual talk about sin. Who among church camp goers does not have a memorable story to tell? My standout memory from that week was one of the songs played over the loudspeaker before morning vespers: "Closer to Fine" by the Indigo Girls. My mind jolted: *WAIT. Aren't these LESBIANS?!?! This song is LIFE GIVING! These are LIFE GIVING LESBIANS!!*

I didn't even know this was a thing or that it could happen in a church setting. I was confused and startled and happy.

Shortly after I got back from that North Carolina youth-with-a splash-of-Indigo-Girls-camp experience, my dad came home from their church one Sunday and announced, "We need to worship together as a family." What he meant was, "We will all start going to the same church and it will be our church." I was still allowed to go to the youth group at the Presbyterian Church, but on Sunday mornings I would be reassigned to my seat in their congregation. But most people didn't sit for long. This was a full gospel wave-your-hands-in-the air-like-you-just-don't-care, Kleenex on the stage, shofar-blowing kind of church.

I thought my mom and dad had lost their ever-loving minds.

But I went out of obedience and became a regular attender. And wow, was I a fish out of living water.

It was a drastic shift in doctrine. Instead of discussing the possibility of gays in the pulpit, people were asking me why I had not been "baptized in the Holy Spirit." Instead of hymns or the Indigo Girls, there were hour-long segments of the service dedicated to singing praise and worship music. Banners were raised. There was clapping and dancing and prophecy. And people fell over after being prayed for. There was a sharp focus on the Second Coming of Christ. As in, it was talked about as if He might be coming back some time before next service. Every week.

The message I got loud and clear was that my faith was way behind and missing a few key ingredients, and I better get them—stat! The stakes were high and hot as literal Hell.

And here's where it got especially tricky for me: I went from entertaining astronautical grand ideas about what I was going to make of my life to learning that, since I was female, there was already a life plan laid out for me. I was taught that the truest way I could honor God was to be a wife and a mother, to set aside anything that wouldn't allow me to fulfill that to a *Southern Living* maxim. I was taught that the Bible was literal and that it clearly instructed me to submit to my future husband, but with those verses that extol husbands and wives to submit to each other not being discussed. I was so confused. Still not really knowing who I was and still eager to please please please, plus being under the weight of fear-based theology, I found a way to shrink my brain into this way of thinking. Hook, line, and sinker. I repented for a worldview that included a place for everyone in the Kingdom of Heaven. I broke up with my boyfriend because we were "unequally yoked." I even threw away my Indigo Girls CDs—including the autographed one— because though God loved the sinner, He hated the sin of homosexuality and I was being an audience for sinfulness.

I took big gulps of the Kool-Aid from that church pretty early on.

I wasn't the only one. My parents dived in, too. I even remember my mom sewing a sequined banner that read "Shekinah Glory" (meaning the glory of God).

It's so strange for me to consider now, how devoted I became and how I thought it meant chucking out parts of the traditions I had experienced until then. There was this "one-up" mentality of our superiority over the "dry" churches. There was an overtold joke at the end of long services when it appeared that the Holy Spirit was on the loose, as evidenced by people running literal laps around the sanctuary or breaking out in holy laughter. The pastor would encourage us, "I'd rather have a little wildfire than no fire at all!" And the reinvigorated crowd would press into that final surge of their hour of power. It was an all-out, middle of the day rave. Meanwhile, my old church friends were not only home from service but from lunch after the service. I was taught that I was getting more of God where I was, and soon I found my foot stuck in the spring trap of self-righteousness.

I was there for it. And so was a super cute boy named Ben, by the way. I went to a few of the youth services, but most of the kids had been on the straighter and narrower since they were small and so were a tight-knit group. I was definitely an outsider, so I just worked to get my head around what they seemed to believe effortlessly. As part of initiation into their crew, I needed to get a token of membership.

Most girls had "True Love Waits" rings on and I came to understand that my body was a source of lust and could not be trusted, so I solidified my partnership with shame around that. But NO WORRIES! Even though I was "tarnished," I found out I could become a "spiritual virgin." (Please quote me a passage regarding this.) And voila! Clean again! I learned there was no quota on grace but also none for fear. Motivated by the latter and desperately aware of my need for the former, I "rededicated my life" at least monthly. Backslidden believers also had no place in the Kingdom of Heaven and the place of their fate was painted clearly.

They had lots of ways to remind us of it.

There was a particular skit that had a lasting impression on me. It's about some kids going to a football game or school dance or something. The place is not the point. It's what happens on the way to their event. There is one kid in the car who feels led to share Jesus with the other kids in the car but he isn't brave enough to witness to them. Tragically, they end up in a car crash together, never having heard the gospel message. The believer lives, but his unsaved friends go to Hell. After the funeral scene in which the saved kid is covered in grief along with guilt over the eternal consequences of his silence about Christ, there is a scene about Hell. I have a vivid memory of one of the kids in the youth group literally pounding her fist on the steps of the stage and screaming that she could hear the "cries and gnashing of teeth from the depths of Hell." You better believe I rededicated every bit of my life at the end of that traumatic Sunday evening.

I was constantly preoccupied by the possibility of a fiery forever.

And I had a haunting rendition of what I thought Hell was like. There is a scene in the movie *Indiana Jones and the Temple of Doom* that played on loop in the back of my mind and was often featured in my nightmares. It terrorized me for years and sometimes still haunts me. In the film, there is a man who is insubordinate in some way and who is brought to the leader of the tribe who is wearing a horned headpiece. His minions are distinguished with tribal paint of white cheeks with black and red stripes. They bring out a cage for the man to be chained inside of. The man is petrified, with wide eyes and his mouth open but mute. Before the leader closes the door on the confined man, he plucks the man's still-beating heart from his chest with his bare hands. It's horrifying. The crowd is cheering. The cage door is shut, and the men begin to position the cage over a fire. The chains of the cage are held in place with skull heads. The dying captive, witnessing his own heart in the hands of his executor, finds his voice only to presumably beg for his life. They flip the cage over so the now heartless but still living man can clearly see his fate as they open the sliding door to a firepit. More chanting. The cage slowly lowers so that the man can be engulfed by unimaginable fear before he is dipped into a lava-like lake of fire. And eventually he is swallowed up by excruciating death. The chanting is celebratory now. Moments go by and the cage is lifted. Charred and empty.

This visual is what my mind still sees today when someone talks about Hell. It is traumatizing. And highly motivating. I wanted to make sure all my religious bases were covered so I'd have the best chance at avoiding such a fate. Next on my list of unmet conditions: speaking in tongues.

I experienced what is known as being baptized in the Holy Spirit somewhere between my sophomore and junior year in college. If you're not familiar with what this entails, it can look like a lot of different things. For me, I completely fell out. Or did I just know to fall to the floor on cue? It's hard to say. Both have happened to me. Anyway, there I was on the floor. And then under a blanket. At my church, if you fell out, you got an airplane grade blanket laid over you. Those were first come first serve, so you may have been counted as extra blessed if you got laid out early enough to get one. Anyway, I'm lying there, hoping for this visitation from heaven to give supernatural utterance to my sinful lips. I wanted this language as evidence that I was seen and held by a God who would give me a secret language to speak to him. Also, I figured if I got it, it would be an assurance that I might make it into Heaven despite myself and my sins. I laid there with anticipation. Nothing. More waiting. More nothing. Then a woman with a sweet smile bent near me and said, "Just make something up, like a jump start, and it will eventually take off from there." Exhausted and disheartened from the fruitless wait, I did just that. I squinted my eyes and began to speak. I'm not sure what jibber I jabbered, but it felt like Pee Wee Herman: "Meka leka hi meka hiney ho!" Whatever it was must've satisfied my onlookers. They congratulated me on "getting it," helped me back up and led me to my seat.

By grace, I was able to see past the absolute weirdness of that induction experience. I could sense the earnest efforts of the church women who wanted me to receive my prayer language. And I trusted God and assumed He would give it to me when I had earned and deserved it.

Turns out, I eventually did speak in tongues. I'm not sure what hurdle I cleared for it to download, but it came. And I used it often. And it was real. I prayed in this mysterious prayer language all the time, on my back deck with no one around and in the car when I was driving by myself. No audience. No pressure. No fireworks. Just me and this dialogue with the Divine.

As my world continued to open up to include encounters with different kinds of people, I found myself so intrigued about how they encountered God, but my fear for their salvation quashed any real chance of relationship with them. I was on a mission. I'd been recruited by God and I was on a direct sales salvation trip. You know how when you're talking to one of the network marketing people who pretend like they're having a conversation with you, but they just want there to be a pause in the conversation long enough for them to interject something about their company's new protein shake or eye cream? I was always waiting for the moment of pause to pronounce the gospel, to make sure everyone around me was safe in the arms of God. It was well-meaning but really obnoxious.

I became so ingrained in the ingrown world of my religion that I missed the face of God all around me for so long.

But not forever.

CAMPING

I love camping. The planning, the prepping, the packing. I love finding the perfect spot, a combination of cleared space and sprawling trees, hopefully by some water. I love watching Ben cook over the open fire. I even love the strong smell of charcoal that veils our sleeping bags and the earthy scent of my girls' skin when they've slept under the sky.

Several years ago on Mother's Day, we were hanging out in the front yard when Celia and Annie proudly presented me with a heavy rectangle box. I could tell by their eyes that they knew I'd love their gift to me. My then five-year-old tried to throw me off the scent by assuredly telling me, "Mama, it is NOT a tent." The look of disbelief and disgust in her older sister's voice ("Annieeeeee-uuhhhhhh!!!") and by the way Ben half-laughed as he hung his head enlightened me that I just might be getting ready to, in fact, receive a tent. And it sure was. Despite the last-minute surprise hijack by the littlest Hardin, I was thrilled and ready to get it and us out into nature.

Ben always goes big with gifts (as he does with just about everything in life), so even though we're a family of four, this was a six-person tent. And because two of the four of us were at that time under four feet tall, it was like an outdoor suite. Ben is not as into the whole camping thing as much as me, so the girls and I have enjoyed a lot of Mama-Daughter campouts in our day. Celia and I especially love an overnight campout at a nearby park, just the two of us.

I have so many sweet memories of her and I building fires and roasting marshmallows, taking nighttime walks and sharing our hearts, waking up to the sound of birds and the brush of the breeze against our brow. We fall asleep talking about God and the sky and the stars and how it was all set in motion. I'm usually up a bit before her, listening to her lightly come into the morning. She wakes to me stroking her hair out of her eyes as I study the replica of her daddy's nose and soft freckles. We slowly make our way onto the dewy grass and rub our sleepy eyes awake to greet the sun. We look around for clues of any night noises that stirred us. (Ahh, yes. *That was a raccoon and yes, he did eat our donuts!!*) There's usually a family of ducks gliding along the water on those outings when we camp by the shore of Lake Shelby. I freeze frame these moments in my Mama Mind as they are almost perfect.

I love everything about those campout nights and the splendor of the following mornings. That is, everything but packing up. That life-sized tent, complete with what seems like three hundred eighty-seven pegs, has never once managed to fold back up to its original shape since I first unpacked it. It's not for lack of trying. Celia and I would lay the expanse of the tan tent out flat and diligently follow the instructions to fold the corners in, creating triangles that were supposed to "easily" fold into other triangles and eventually somehow end up in a nice taut rectangle of compacted canvas that we could just slip back into the bag and effortlessly zip up. Easy peasy tent origami.

Except it has never been that easy.

We'll start out with tenacity, but within minutes, we're making strange grunting sounds (and truth be told, I am likely cursing under my breath). Usually at some point, I'll have Celia sit on the wadded-up tent to compress it enough to possibly shove it back into the stuff sack. I recall that we got it in for the most part after our first campout. I'm not sure the sack was zipped up all the way, but all the parts made it in, and my protruding veins didn't actually pop out of my strained neck, so I counted that as a win. With each use, it seems harder to get that tent to fit back into its case. Over time, we've just started sort of draping the mangled material between the handles of the case and carrying it like a messy tent purse, tent parts spilling out everywhere. The last time we camped with that thing, I'd had it. We literally just loosely wrangled it up and threw it and the remaining tent pegs that hadn't been lost in transit into the back of the truck. It was never going back into its original container.

My spiritual journey has been like that tent.

At first, it was all put together and neatly packaged. And it stayed just so for a long while. But each time I would encounter something broader than my tradition, the sphere of my soul would expand to include the possibility of a God who was bigger than I had been trained to imagine. In what I thought was true Jesus-following fashion, I'd go home and feverishly try to fit everything neatly back into its intact and tightly sealed theology.

It's important to note that I wanted my God to fit back into His place in my tiny mind. It would bring me comfort. I love neat, clean lines and I feel safe in certitude. But you can't dismiss people groups because they are "non-Christians," especially when you recognize the face of God in them. You can't make broad sweeping statements about subjects when you realize you've only studied them completely subjectively. You can't un-encounter things or eradicate experiences no matter what size your tent is.

Like . . .

When we've traveled to countries where the presets and postures toward God look distinctly different than ours. And still beautifully so.

When I've felt equally awed by the presence of God at a Catholic Mass, on a trail run through the woods, in a counseling session, and on the sands of Thailand.

When I met my friend's relative, a Methodist minister. And a woman. And a lesbian.

When I just sat around and wondered, "What else will I discover?" Like when early Christians learned their flat earth was really round and that the firmament was not in fact a solid ceiling but rather a wide-open space.

When I started considering the existence of Christ before the man, Jesus, came to Earth. And since then, His resurrection and beyond.

I just couldn't make the faith of my formative years fit back into the package of fundamentalism.

When I see the footprints and fingerprints of God all around me and the face of God where I didn't expect to.

When I meet people from a few states north of my hometown who have never spent a Sunday morning in any of the ways I had and who kindly wondered aloud, "You guys really believe that stuff about . . . (insert a dozen things we actually believed)?"

When I've encountered total peace and newfound embodiment on the yoga mat, which I had been taught was an altar to other gods and therefore should be off limits for any true Christian.

After a lineup of life experiences that widened my mind and wrecked my theology, I just couldn't make the faith of my formative years fit back into the package of fundamentalism. Like the tent, it just stopped fitting back into the bag.

UNRAVELING CONVERSATION

"How do you make God the boss of your life?"

I pumped the brakes as my eyes shot to the booster seat in the back, where the question had come from five-year-old Celia's lips.

There was this autopilot response that rose up from within me like a prepared monologue (or in this case, a gospel tract). My mouth started to form familiar words. Instead, I clumsily but insistently urged her,

"Whatever you do baby, don't just say something that someone tells you to say."

I was caught off guard by my own reaction. I dialed back my unanticipated fear and brought my answer down to her heart's level. I had an eagerness for her to understand that talking to God was less about a dutiful proclamation and more about a continual conversation between the two of them. I wanted to make sure that she knew there was no exact thing her mouth had to mimic. I did not want to parent her in her faith by simply listing prerequisites for a punched ticket to Heaven.

My desire was for her to know from the beginning that faith was not just about membership induction. It is about participation, that she is a part of God and that God is a part of her the same way she and I are a part of each other, but on a much more intimate and yet grander scale.

My reaction in that moment with Cel was the beginning of an inner dialogue that has been going on inside me since then. Truly, the exchange within my core had been whispering to me for a few years before, but this talk with her turned up the dial and I knew I had to listen to my own questions.

She was coming to me with curiosity and looking for certainty.

My certainty was in the midst of unraveling because of my curiosities.

It was an interesting and even inconvenient time for my creed to begin to crumble.

Our belief system can be predicated around a single issue, like the Sinner's Prayer. We can live our entire lives with our eyes set on the reward of that recitation, keeping our telescopic sight honed in on the target of an eternity of tomorrows in Heaven. However, if we allow elements in our periphery to enter into view, the scope of our world expands outside of the lens through which we've been trained to see things. It is then that our faith becomes not just about a system but also about a culmination of our experiences that are formative to our faith. We can begin to see a bird's eye view of things now, taking in sights that we couldn't (or wouldn't or didn't want to) see before.

My beliefs had recently encountered reformation as my travels, experiences, and relationships had begun to reshape my convictions. I'd been living in my head about all of it for a few years and now, and at Celia's promptings, I had to begin to sort through things.

I wondered: how many of my spiritual answers are not really my own?

How many things had I simply regurgitated?

What did I really believe . . . about anything? About everything?

I didn't question whether God was real, but I did call into question the only story of God I'd ever been told.

I felt like the Image of God had been baked down like a Shrinky Dink, so small that I could fit Him into my pocket. But is that all her little mind could hold right now?

I understand that kids need easy-to-follow steps for things before they find their own way. Mystery and abstract and gray . . . they can't understand those just yet. I get it. But I wanted to at least let my girl know God is not like something you learn how to get and then you're done. I wanted her to know that knowing God is about a continuous curiosity and ongoing openness.

I looked for an analogy that might help her understand.

"Remember when you learned your letters? First you learned what they looked like, then what sounds they made. Now you're learning to read by putting words together. God's a little bit like how when we started with the alphabet. We learn a little bit about what God is like. And then we learn what God sounds like in our hearts. And then we learn to read what God is telling us. After that, if we keep going, we learn how to notice the story of God all around us and also inside of us. And it's the most beautiful story we'll ever know."

LEAVING CHURCH

The quarter mile drive to our church drug on like the time between lab tests and diagnosis. I looked down to read the speedometer at twenty-five miles per hour. I simply couldn't press the peddle with enthusiasm.

When I finally slid into the parking lot, I was relieved that I had somehow managed to still be there at 8:30 a.m. on the dot for our scheduled practice time.

I made my ascent to the stage and began to shuffle through the pages of songs, searching a particular one that announced God's "reckless love." I was up for the task. *I can do this*, I thought. I do believe that God's love is reckless, boundless, limitless. We warmed up and ran through that song. My heart expanded. Then the next song. Predictable melody (as with most Christian worship songs). Predictable message: an anthem full of phrases about "Only One Way." My heart constricted.

Listen, I'll sing about God all day long. God's goodness. God's faithfulness. God's mercy. Maybe it's just the expected genre of the thing that gets me. It seemed like there was only one way and one style and one 'brand' we were supposed to market, as if that was the superior way to worship. Maybe it's because I shouldn't belt out exclamations through song when there are so many questions stirring around inside of me. I'm not sure. The only thing I'm certain of is that it became harder for me to do.

I tensed.

I ached.

I shook.

Oh, but I sang.

I sounded certain, assured, convinced.

With every compliment I received after church, I shuddered. *I'm such an imposter.*

I'd like to say that the very moment I could no longer come to terms with this brand of fundamental theology, I cut ties with it. But those bindings were tight. I suppose I kept waiting for the denominational doctrine to broaden alongside my own morphing mindset. Looking back, I see how unfair that was of me. I guess I just so desperately wanted a reason to stay. You see, I really loved these people, and I didn't want to leave them. But I'd show up—amped with anxiety—and sit in the metal folding chair, sweating.

The well-intended words from the pulpit sometimes felt like weapons against people I had come to love. People I had learned to see as part of this bigger family of "us," the ones who used to be "them." As I sat there each Sunday, I felt like I was wearing a wool turtleneck in the dead of July, confined and uncomfortable. God was birthing something new in me, but my spirit compressed inside of this context. This labor was arduous and the pain was awful.

At this point, my faith was equal parts love and fear. It was the fear that kept me showing up as a faithful follower. The overriding terror was of the trap door to Hell opening up beneath me at any moment to swallow me whole if I discarded this culture-bound way to God.

Still, I sang and sat and squirmed for a long while.

Until I just couldn't anymore.

The constructs of this subculture began to collapse beneath my feet.

I cannot do this anymore.
I cannot wear this badge.
I cannot be in this club.
I cannot wave this flag.

So many cannots.

So, what can I do?

The whisper in my spirit now spoke up, sure to be heard this time.

"Well, you can just leave.
No one is making you stay.
You can just go."

And so . . . that's what we did.

PAINT BY NUMBERS

I'm not much of an artist. When Celia was two, she asked me if I could draw her a picture of a cat. My response: "I really actually can't, Baby. People have different giftings and that's just not mine. I mean, I can draw something for you, but I can almost promise it's not gonna end up looking anything like a cat."

I learned early on that I was not going to be an affluent visual artist. In the true fashion of a subscriber to a performance-based belief system of worth, I would choose projects that required little talent so that I could execute well. Paint-by-numbers were my go-to. I loved that I could literally just connect the dots with my crayon and "create" a pretty picture. Several years ago I even went to one of those paint-by-numbers classes for adults, you know, those art and wine nights where the instructor gives you detailed directions and voila!—Her promptings have led you to paint the perfect cow in a pasture. (Of course, I went almost solely for the wine, but I digress.)

Life is much less like a step-by-step process and much more broad strokes of bright, brilliant paint across a page.

My early religion was like a paint-by-number. Predictable and neat, it laid out a well-planned path before me with steps to follow to make it to the finish line: Heaven.

Once you get your passport approved, be obedient and keep your head down.

And that makes nice enough sense for religion.

But after a while, I started to struggle to see how the dots connected.

When I began to realize that we aren't simply here to go through the robotic motions of religion but to actually abide in God, my perspective drastically shifted. I came to understand that Life is much less like a step-by-step process and much more like broad strokes of bright, brilliant paint across a page.

The color spills and splashes outside of the lines.

This dwelling with God explores the corners of the canvas.

And then dissolves the frame because there is no edge to The Spirit.

I've learned "the way" is way out of the lines I'd been so comfortable within.

In fact, now I am realizing that the movement of the Creator is much less manageable. It's as if instead of an even coat of paint on a page, God is more like a drop of ink into water where everything blends together and you can't tell the ink and water apart because they're so melded together and everything is neither and both.

It's magnificent really.

But my handling of it can be messy. Sometimes I wonder if I'm not better at the old way. Chasing the rewards of religion and working toward perfecting patterns. Formula versus flow. I'm a good rule follower when I'm not busy being a system bucker.

I also question, though . . .

Has God been eclipsed by my religion?

Have some of my church experiences been the moon blocking the light of the Sun?

Or have those experiences been like constellations that have in fact been traceable and predictable, and yet beautiful expressions of the God of the universe?

Either way, I'm here now.

I've always been hesitant to write what I "believe" about God because it's ever unfolding. Fixing words on a page doesn't mean my position is fixed. If I'm ever so bound to certainty without holding space for mystery, I'm in trouble.

This whole thing shifts and cycles as I continue to explore and experience.

The point is, it's not frozen. I may later recant some of what I feel so strongly about now.

Also, as I openly grapple with religion and church, I remain respectful of their tenets. I look back on my upbringing with fear and trepidation, yes. But also with fondness and warmth. I can arrange it in my mind to highlight the variables that affected me negatively or the ones that shaped my soul into the sojourner I have become.

In deconstructing some of the trappings of my tradition, I want to be sure to not be caught up in another one, namely the snare of cynicism. Man, it's so easy for someone who speaks sarcasm fluently to throw stones through the stained-glass windows. I don't want to be that. I don't want to hold that in my heart. I don't want to convey that in my words.

Maybe in a few years or even in a few months I will have changed my mind about some of this. And I reserve the right to amend my today position in light of what I may learn tomorrow. The only thing I can't imagine is shrinking back the broadness of God in order to fit back into the places I've passed through, now that the tent has been opened wide and pitched under the vast ether.

OLD JOURNALS

I recently thumbed through some old journals full of prayers—perfectly polished petitions to a seemingly very far off God.

Starched, formal, ornate.

"Oh Most Gracious Father in Heaven . . . "

"Most Great and High Lord . . . "

"Oh Holy and Almighty God Above . . . "

And then I'd proceed with something like,

"I come before your throne . . . " and continue with well-rehearsed recitations and skillful negotiations that I hoped would make it all the way up to the cosmos.

Eventually, I tried on several other greetings, from Yahweh to Daddy God.

And I'd interject those and other names of God an odd number of times throughout my prayers.

"Oh God, thank you, Lord, for all your blessings, Jesus."

(Can you imagine if we did that in actual conversation? We would never do that to say, Jennifer. "Oh Jennifer, thank you, Jen for being my friend, Jenny." It's just weird.)

I named things and claimed things.

I declared deliverance and prophesied promises.

I released blessings and bound up curses.

I prayed for a position of favor with a God I was taught rewarded with healing and prosperity. I prayed to be content behind the curtain of life's stage while the men around me were to be front and center—with their ideas, opinions, and last words. I prayed to be able to keep things and people in their well-organized categories, especially the one about Who's In and Who's Out.

Over time, my mouth stopped being able to utter those prayers that I had struggled with for years. My mind could no longer scale back the Bigger Picture so that I could fit in. My heart longed for a new way to know The Divine. In short, my religion came off the rails.

There was a long period of sitting in silence before God.

Studying.

Searching.

Stretching.

Eventually I again borrowed verbiage to try to pray, this time from Judy Blume.

"Are you there God? It's me, (Melinda)."

(Long pause.)

"I don't even know how to pray anymore . . . not really.

"Everything I've been taught to say sounds manufactured. I feel like I'm navigating a landmine of triggers just trying to talk to you. It's like I'm unlearning how to speak the code of a members-only club I don't belong to anymore. So, I'm just gonna stumble through prayer for a while, okay? Oh and also, the pronoun thing is proving tricky for me lately. I've been taught to know you as He, as Father. And I love that. Still, sometimes, in my most vulnerable moments especially, when I need the more gentle, warm, hair-stroking love of a Mama, I wonder if you might be that, too. Anyway, I want to make sure you know I still love you, even if I don't understand You the way I used to. And I hope that You haven't let go of me."

LABEL

I don't want my struggles with church and my separation from some of my religious heritage to imply an eradication of Jesus from "my heart."

Having said that, if someone were to ask me if I am a Christian, I might stammer a bit.

You see, my answer has largely to do with how the person asking defines the word.

"Christian" has become a reductionist term that encapsulates the context of culture moreso than illustrates a life that reflects the teachings of Jesus. For some, it means that I've made a public profession of faith. For others, it means I'm predestined for eternity with God. For others still, it's about being pro-life and anti-gay. We also have "Christ followers," and so on. If I don't have time to unpack what I mean when I say I'm a Christian, then I just hope I'm not asked.

Then there's the more nuanced and modern version of the question:

"Are you a believer?" Well, a believer in what?

A meek-mannered Jesus who's painted picture looks like your blue-eyed long-haired cousin from the States? No.

A Jesus who would have you shoving your picket sign of hate in someone's face? Uh-uh.

In a Creator whose favorites are the Americans? Especially the white ones? Nope.

That women shouldn't be in the pulpit? No sir.

In a church that doesn't open its doors and leadership opportunities to the LGBTQIA+ community? Hard pass on that.

But if you're asking me if I'm a believer in Jesus, the Living Expression of God, who is the Light who came to shine upon everyone? Yes, absolutely.

Jesus, the confronter of oppressors? I am.

Jesus, the one who called out the religious zealots of his time and who, based on history, would be calling them out today? I am for sure a believer in that guy, yes.

Jesus the feminist? Yep.

Jesus the friend of the marginalized? Yes!

Jesus, the perfect model of compassion? Indeed.

I mean, this is just for starters.

And then when people ask me if we're churchgoers, I get

awkward. Because I feel like that's my cue to offer an excited, "Yes!" But we don't go to church.

Church can be a lot of things.

It can be the place of false advertising with its marquees of "Come as you are" but with the unspoken footnote, "And stay if you are like us."

It can be a place we go to be spoon-fed religion, yet we still leave hungry for Truth.

It can be a refuge that promises light but carries the heavy weight of some things done in the dark.

Even still, church can be a beautiful shape-shifting community and a deeply meaningful well of growth. It has been that for me at times. Maybe there will be another chapter in life where it is that for me again. The lump that I get in my throat when I consider it tells me that it may be way off if so. It's true that I may be a bit wary of it and on some darker days perhaps even a bit suspicious. However, I do remain open to the possibility.

I don't want to be unkind toward church. Church offered me a story of Jesus. And it loved me well in its ways. It showed me a way to God. But maybe I was looking for something at church that I was never meant to find there. I'm not sure. For now, I'm seeking God in my yellow velvet chair in the early morning moments as I sit quietly and sip my coffee. Our family sometimes has "church" at the lake, as we rest in tree hammocks and take in Creation. Fellowship happens around dinner tables or on afternoon walks. Because if God is everywhere, then church can be everywhere, too.

It's hard for me to give one-word answers in response to questions that are as layered as geology or even just baklava. Especially when I'm still working my way toward the answers.

"Out beyond ideas of wrongdoing and rightdoing,
there is a field. I'll meet you there.
When the soul lies down in that grass,
the world is too full to talk about.
Ideas, language, even the phrase "each other"
doesn't make any sense.
The breeze at dawn has secrets to tell you.
Don't go back to sleep.
You must ask for what you really want.
Don't go back to sleep.
People are going back and forth across the doorsill
where the two worlds touch.
The door is round and open.
Don't go back to sleep."
—Rumi, "A Great Wagon"[8]

Eclipsed by My Own Life

I bet you've got some things in your life that you don't remember ever signing up for. But once they are part of your life, they can be a little hard to renegotiate. Maybe it's the job you sorta kinda bumped into, but now it seems essential to the health of your bank account. Maybe it's an endeavor that you didn't mean to turn into the behemoth it is now, but friendly monster it is, and it demands to be fed. Often. Maybe it's a friendship or an obligation, but the distinctive mark here is that these things all look like good things. Things you should want to do. Things you should be proud of.

But something's missing. Something still stays in the shadow, in spite of all the sunlight.

Sometimes moving into your own true light is knowing when other good light isn't yours. Not really. Even when your name got assigned to it. Even when you're pretty good at it. It might just not be your truest light.

GOLDEN HANDCUFFS

The chicken Cordon bleu is still frozen in the middle and the vegetable medley is begging for seasoning. I inwardly complain, "You'd think the food would be better considering the ice sculpture in the middle of the appetizer table. There's someone else's lipstick mark on the ring of my glass. (Cue gag.) Gross.

I excuse myself from this never-ending awards banquet to "use the restroom" and sneak outside for a smoke. It's a bitingly cold January day and my gloved hands are struggling to wind the red Bic lighter. I hesitantly take off the thumb of my left glove and manage to set my cigarette aflame. I suck in a big drag but can't tell exactly when to stop blowing it out. Is that still smoke or just the cold air? Even though I'm freezing, I finish it almost to the filter and stomp it out with my worn out Nine West sale rack pumps. I open the door to go back inside— but first, a generous amount of Bath and Body Works Vanilla Bean lotion. Because obviously a smell-good lotion makes for a smell-good smoker. (Eye roll.)

My steps are slow heading back in to meet my work team.

I hate meetings.

And banquet halls.

And uncomfortable shoes.

But I do love (most of) the people surrounding me at that table.

I just feel like I'm definitely out of place.

While the director deliberately delays the announcing of the award winners to build up our suspense, I daydream about a life outside of these golden handcuffs.

What would I do if I were brave?

I'm jolted out of my trance when I hear my name, "Melinda Mathis!"

My tablemates enthusiastically clap and congratulate me. I won!! Because I'm not intently listening to the presentation, I'm not exactly sure what my actual award is, but I paint on a wide smile, and bounce my way to the stage to receive it.

It's one of those exchanges where you shake one hand and take your plaque with the other. And that's where the moment starts to go in slow motion. I feel like I am watching overhead and seeing myself hand over my heart for a pawn. I know that sounds dramatic, but I was in my early twenties, so a lot of things in my head sounded that way, but also like truth. I should be thrilled by this moment. Even sort of proud. Instead, I feel conflicted. Here I am getting rewarded for a job well done. I mean, I had done a good job. But for what? All of this work that I am pouring my energy into is meaningless to me. I'm good at it because I'm a pleaser. Not because I care about what I'm doing. Is this the rest of my life? More years logged at a job I don't love just because someone thinks I do it well? More suiting up for the charade instead of admitting I am yearning for something different? And the big one: More time spent trading in my passions for a paycheck?

Snap! Back into the actual moment. I take the plaque. And the fat check that comes with it. I sit down oddly disappointed. But as often happens, those dollar signs in the now unsealed envelope keep me in my seat.

And at that job "people would die to have."

The success I'd achieved for Corporate America came at the cost of realizing the triumphs of my own dreams. And so along I went, the puppet on a string.

For another decade.

By then, I had received accolades, sales quota trips, and bonuses in my pharmaceutical sales job that were as big as my first salary. And they felt unearned. I don't mean to underplay my hand. I was good at my job. It's just that . . . it felt like someone else's success. Every time I was awarded for something, it was like a reminder that I was detained in a life that made all material sense for someone else while my real life was out there, waiting for me to show up and live it. I was yearning for a sense of purpose. Every day I felt like an imposter. I'd hop in my company car, wearing my boutique-bought outfit and head to clients before our team met for a "lunch meeting" at the sushi bar. And then there was the guilt. Someone would die for this job, yet it's mine and I'd die for a chance at something else, but I'm too afraid I'd lose my cushy life trying.

It was at a retirement party for a colleague where I came to the realization that I was paving the way to my own retirement party. That was the trajectory of things, to be sure. During a congratulatory toast under the clinking sound of the glasses and "cheers," I looked at Ben and whispered, "This can't be my life. I cannot do this anymore. If I give more years to this company and retire from here with a boatload of money, it will have cost me my very soul."

He said, "Quit. We'll figure it out."

And I did. It took a few more months, but I eventually cut loose from those golden handcuffs. With little plan of what to do next, I leapt. I threw on my favorite jeans and a tank top, grabbed the keys to our 1975 wood panel station wagon, turned the dial 'til I found a station I loved, and sang a song of freedom to the top of my lungs as I set out to find the thing that had been hidden in the shadow of someone else's success. I had given myself permission to create my own.

HARVEST

This part is hard for me to write about. I still haven't processed it all yet. I tried something. It didn't work. It still stings.

Here's what happened:

Harvest Coffee & Cafe was a little spot we owned for just around four years. The daydream grew out of some jotted notes on a half-page of paper and a single recipe that people raved over. Some notes and a salad. That's it. I'd had the idea for a while about a cozy spot where people could gather for good coffee, healthy food, and rich conversation. I was content to let it be just that, an idea. The thought of actually running a restaurant seemed like a bit much. At the time, my stress level was exactly two on a scale of one to ten. After a serendipitous introduction by one of my past doctor-clients to a patient of his who owned a blue-collar company, I had scored the chance to actually develop and run a wellness program for his employees. I loved my work and the flexibility of my schedule. I was blogging, growing the wellness program, and seeing individual and family clients as I could. In essence, I was experiencing authentic success for the first time ever. Living my best life. Things were smooth sailing. Even still, we convinced ourselves to give this cafe a shot. My biggest draw toward it was the idea of creating a place of community within the hometown we'd come to love so much. That draw coupled with Ben's three-steps-ahead-of-me enthusiasm, and we opened.

I think they call it naivete.

I had no clue what I was about to enter into.

From the moment we opened, I was overwhelmed. The learning curve was exhausting. We had enough sense to hire people with more industry experience than I did who managed and cooked, which was anyone with any. We scored some wins and losses on this front, and the emotional and financial toil was staggering.

I did not feel like a success.

Everything about this place felt like hanging on for dear life to get the next plate filled and the next bill paid. I wasn't sure who I was in this space, so I let myself be tossed by the changing public perspective about everything from menu options to open hours. I allowed the weight of opinion to press down on my shoulders 'til they slumped.

Sure, I wanted to please our customers. But I still longed for more than their good reviews of our chicken salad. I needed our work to count for more.

An idea came to me like a lightning bolt. What if we offered a 'Pay What You Can' model one day each week? I remember telling Ben. He pointed out every reason this was crazy and then asked when we should start. So, we did. All of our offerings on Wednesdays cost customers just what they had or wanted to pay. My heart would burst at the start of those days.

Around the same time, we added to that a 'Pay It Forward' board where customers could gift community members a coffee or lunch or what have you. I just needed something to be outside of just us and part of the bigger picture.

A few months after that, we started having farm-to-table dinners, four-course meals sourced from our local farmers that folks enjoyed while gathered with friends, new and old. I'd sit back and listen to the laughter as friendships formed between guests who hadn't met until those nights. *Yes*, I thought. *This is it*. This is the community I was hoping to create.

Those three elements with community at their core were the true successes of Harvest. Still, the writing was on the wall.

We weren't actually making it. No ledger showed any financial wins. Hell, we barely broke even some months and were at a loss at the end of others.

During this time, my Tito's game was strong and my stress level turned sips into gulps. When I finally sobered up, closing became the only thing to do. I could see clearly that the chapter was complete. We likely even wrote a few pages too many. And you know, closing was a part of the success as well. I was no longer motivated by pride to stay open just because I didn't want to wave the flag of defeat in the middle of Main Street. So, we did what was right for me and Ben and for our family. Even though I knew it was time to let it go, there was heartbreak in it for sure. More bitter than sweet to stay open, more sweet than bitter to close, but still a mix of both.

There were lots of both/ands . . .

Success. Failure.

Giving. Receiving.

Treasure. Treachery.

Numbing. Feeling.

Pace. Patience.

Dreaming. Dissolving.

Community. Self.

About a year after we closed, Ben and I got a letter about the cafe.

"We just want to thank you for having a desire to create an atmosphere to bring people together as a community. You both are so brave and strong and full of ideas. You have been gifted to create something out of nothing and make it beautiful. The testimony and season of Harvest yielded rich relationships that continue to this day. Nothing will ever be wasted. You make new roads and clear new paths so that people can experience beauty and freshness. Your ideas are so big that people start to dream after hearing them. The seeds you have planted will have a great harvest."

We were a success after all, I suppose. I'm still sorting through what this chapter in our lives meant. But I do know that, in spite of the business mistakes and challenges and naivete and all the rest, knowing that people found community in it makes the lessons worth it.

Our recipe for our famous Harvest Salad,
the one that started the dream:

HARVEST SALAD:

3 gala apples, diced small
3 cups broccoli, chopped small
1 1/2 cups edamame
1 1/2 cups seedless red grapes
1/2 cup dried cranberries
3 stalks celery, thinly sliced
1 cup salted roasted cashews

DRESSING:

1/2 cup evoo
3 tbsp red wine vinegar
3 cloves garlic, crushed & minced
1/2 tsp yellow mustard
1 1/2 tsp celery seed
1/2 tsp salt

Enjoy!

GROUNDED

As soon as I walked into her office, I knew I was in the right place. I sat down on her couch and mentally giggled to myself. The whole couch and therapist thing took some time for me to get used to but years ago I had. I find that there have been seasons when offering myself a gift of some good and wise counsel has been life-giving. It had been years since I found myself across from a professional therapist and I was instantly grateful to have met Jeannine. Her smile and curls were soft and her countenance calming. I was at ease with her right away.

Which was a good thing because it all went woo woo within ten minutes:

Her: "Do you have any pain . . . Like chronic pain in your body?"

Me: "Yes. In my feet—" The expression that crossed her face melted my words. She already knew.

Her: "Yes, I'm getting a sense that something inside of you is asking for groundedness and your body is trying to tell you that. Your feet are literally trying to root."

Tears rushed to my eyes. How did she know? This woman did not know who I was or anything about me or anything about our life circumstances. It felt like God was speaking through her voice and pointedly but softly advising me to take note of what my body was begging for. It felt like the prophecies that came forth on Sunday mornings from growing up. It was an oracle four years in the making.

Four years earlier, we were just about to finish up all the renovation on our loft in downtown Shelbyville. As we moved closer and closer to moving in, a strange thing started happening. I began to have dreams about strangers being in my house. I did not know a single person in my dreams, but they were all houseguests of mine. It was a warning of sorts about what would be just around the corner for us.

We were able to finally move into our loft and get settled. The second floor of our building had two sides; we lived in one and built out a two-bedroom apartment across the hall. Airbnb was fairly new and we took a stab at it by placing the smaller one online. And on a whim, we threw up a listing for our side, our home, thinking we might rent it out for the Kentucky Derby or an occasional weekend. It could be fun!

We slapped on a price tag to make it worth the while if we ever had to uproot for a weekend here or there and hit "Submit" on the website. Never in our wildest dreams could we have imagined what would come next. Almost immediately, we got a request for visitors to come and stay in our side of the building. Our home. And then more requests came. And more. In a year's time, from that very first rental, we found ourselves having to come up with our own accommodations constantly between April and the beginning of December, as strangers moved into our home for the weekend or even full weeks. No exaggeration. And the two-bedroom began to rent as well. We were vagabonds. We would wake up on Thursday morning and scramble to figure out what we were going to do for accommodations. It started to feel less fun and more interruptive for me and the girls.

Feel me here. We had to load up our suitcases and kids and ready the house for incoming strangers almost every week. Think cleaning out the refrigerator, switching out bedding, tucking away the girls' artwork that enjoyed only a three-day exhibit, shoving odds and ends that didn't make it to their proper place into the one locked closet before check-in. All the while I was hoping (and often failing) to remember to grab everything we might need for school, sports, sleepovers.

Where would we go this time? Some weeks were so bananas we'd be making reservations as we pulled away from Main Street, uncertain where to land. We'd stay in some cool spots a short drive from town. One summer we toggled back and forth between our loft and a camper we rented and parked at the lake, just about a mile from home. Another month we stayed at the same hotel three weekends in a row and the valet service let us keep our bikes parked there since we'd be back in just a few days. We had family sleepovers with friends every now and then and of course there was always a warm welcome at my parents' house.

We couldn't plan play dates or slumber parties or host friends for dinner without consulting the reservation calendar. The girls had to keep their rooms "renter friendly," so there could be no kid posters on the walls or personalization. Everything was filtered through how it would affect our guests.

I think I knew cognitively and logistically what the back and forth would be like. But I couldn't project what this would do to me on every other level.

My soul would go through this severing.

Not because strangers were in our home.

But because I started to feel strange in our home.

I know, I know, this sounds fun for some people, loaded with spontaneity and a seeming vacation every weekend. I salute them.

For me, this retelling ties my stomach in knots.

From the business side alone, it was a huge success. Our reservations were increasingly full. But that success eclipsed our needs as a family as we were held captive by the calendar.

The freedom we had initially, eventually felt like chains. I came to dread and resent every time the app notification sounded. What now? Do we have to leave again?

My wanderlust husband seemed to thoroughly enjoy the unfettered nature of what was rocking me to the core. I'm a bird with a wide wingspan and I love to fly free, but I also need a nest. I think he could live out of a suitcase and be completely content, but the girls and I started to crave and then ache for sacred space. Just a place where all four Hardins have a favorite spot on our couch, a place to hang our backpacks or car keys (even if the actual hanging up part evades us), where echoes of laughter bounce off our walls and where we all have a seat at the dinner table where we unpack our days together and I nourish their bellies while we fill up on the soul food of connection.

But we didn't have that.

Instead, we were renting out our life.

I wish that I could tell you that I was the happy-go-lucky-live-out-of-a-suitcase, "As long as I'm with you, babe, I'm home," kinda girl. Some days I can be that. Other times I'm whiny because I forgot my flip-flops and my book is by my actual bedside and my Q-tips did not make it into my suitcase again and I have to stop by CVS for the third time to replace the toothbrush that I seem to keep forgetting to pack.

I wish I could tell you that I managed all of this seamlessly and with grace and patience and effortless rhythm. But I can't tell you that. It's not my truth. It feels like I'm complaining about something that was blessedly bringing our family income and adventure. What kind of ungrateful jerk do you have to be to not appreciate that?

Well, maybe an honest one. Maybe one that knows herself better now. Maybe one who is learning to not apologize for what she needs, even when the opportunity and the lifestyle seem enticing.

At the end of our second year as vagabonds, Celia said, "Mama, I know this isn't really like our real home. Because ya know, the renters and all. And that's okay. But it does make me have a question. If *this* isn't home, where *is* home?"

My answer was well crafted and believable about home being where we were all gathered, and the foundation of it was love and each other. I hoped that we would both latch onto the sentiment.

The real answer evaded me. I'm not sure where home is. Where to settle. Where to ground. But now even my body was begging to know.

And four years into this lifestyle, I found myself sitting in my brand-new therapist's office, talking about the pain in my unrooted feet.

At Jeannine's suggestion, I began the practice of sitting at the base of a tree to gather its grounding energy. I know it sounds crazy, but some days it saved my life. My seat on the earth's grass and my back against the strong trunk, I would trace the exposed roots with my fingers as Creation's vibrations flowed like electricity through my body.

At one appointment with Jeannine, she gifted me with a tiny watercolor she had painted. It was a tree. The two-by-two frame was small enough to place into overnight bags, and I'd set it out on the nightstand of wherever our heads would land when we had renters at our loft. That way, when I couldn't find a tree to nestle up against, I would at least have a rendition of one to remind me of what it had come to mean to me, a reminder of how it feels to be held by the Holder of all things.

It was such a kind gesture. And it centered me in moments. As grateful as I was for the advice and the gift, I was still longing for a real place to drop my real roots. We all need roots, to be rooted in what's true. My true roots are that I need a place to be planted.

About a year ago, we drove by a house where the For Sale sign had just been planted. When we pulled into the driveway of this little ranch, Ben had the entire exterior artfully reconceived before I could even get the lockbox opened. Once inside, our ideas swirled. If there had been any lingering questions about whether this was our next home, those would have been settled the moment I saw the tree through the living room window.

We all need roots, to be rooted in what's true.

It was majestic. And a replica of the painted tree in the small frame from Jeannine. In an instant, I felt the pain in my feet relax. I could sink my soul into this place, root here in this house. It answered the primal call in me that had been longing for home. Before I knew it, I noticed that my hands were raised in a posture of praise and a hallelujah sounded in my spirit.

It had taken Ben a while to truly realize the stress that being optionally homeless was causing us, but he came to understand that my heart couldn't keep pace with so many open doors. I think coming through the temporary doors of wherever we were staying one night and seeing three tear-streaked faces was the clencher. The girls and I were desperate for a sacred space and a sense of stability. And so began the official search for a new Hardin address, one that belonged to just us. No Airbnb, just home.

When we told the girls about our upcoming move and we saw the light on their faces eclipse the weariness from wandering, Ben understood what we were giving them. What we were giving us.

All the dominoes fell into place and we were at the closing table less than two weeks later. It was ours! Of course, we can never leave well enough alone. Sledgehammers were flying that same day as we began to transform the space into our personal sanctuary. B was reconfiguring the floorplan and I was picturing family hang time around the kitchen table and out in the backyard.

We spent the next several months renovating the dated interior into the midcentury modern design we'd been mentally drooling over. There'd be days I'd show up and just sit on the floor and look out the picture window at that tree—my tree—and worship would envelope my senses, overcome by it all.

Nomadic existence had its moments, but nothing compares to a sense of refuge only home can offer.

I am rich with gratitude.

The framed picture of the painted tree from Jeanine sits on a small table next to the mustard yellow velvet chair in our front room. I can see both the real tree and the painted version from the same vantage point. It serves as a reminder of faithfulness and provision. It reminds me to speak up on my own behalf about what I need. And it prompts me to plop down by my actual tree and let the earth's cushion hold me close, at home and at home.

ALMOST

I never wanted to be Joanna Gaines.

When we bought the downtown buildings in our hometown of Shelbyville with the idea of turning an upstairs space into our home, people thought we were crazy to try to pull it off. At several points along the way, we agreed with them. Until we did it. The results eclipsed even our wildest dreams. Making a big move in the middle of town attracts varying opinions. There were fans of our local projects and those less enthused with our work. We've learned that it's dangerous to put stock in publicity about us, good or bad. All in all, some days it's best for us to go about our work with our heads down so our motives stay pure, and we aren't distracted by whatever chorus is singing the loudest. We don't want to drown in a sea of opinions while we're working to keep these buildings afloat. But it was exciting that our story got to be part of an overarching narrative that was being rewritten on the streets of Shelbyville.

The thing about a good storyline is that it can be the one told on repeat. And ours was: how we were among a small crew of catalysts behind the revitalization of the nucleus of Main Street. It was an honor to be included alongside Ben in the anecdotes for sure. After all, it was a partnership and even more, a family affair, but he was the forerunner in this endeavor. And so, the acclaim for me felt undeserved in a lot of ways. Still, it seems to be the front-page news of our personal story.

We did garner some local media recognition during the renovation process, but that never prepared us for what was on the horizon. We had rented one of our lofts for the weekend to a literary agent who had worked on some projects with the Senior Vice President of Entertainment for a production company. The agent had told her about our loft spaces and before we knew it, we were on a Skype call about the possibility of filming a home renovation show. In a matter of months, we were filming what's called a sizzle reel, a five-ish minute synopsis of us, our story, and work to date. A couple of months after that, we got a greenlight to begin filming a pilot for HGTV. In a whirlwind, we turned another dilapidated old building into a home.

Logistically, the project was exasperating. A rehab that would have typically taken a year to complete was miraculously done in ten tumultuous weeks. Don't believe the television timeline for a second. I mean, we did it. And by "we" I mean every single contractor we knew plus any willing soul who had a hammer and a heart to help. We were thrilled with the end result! But to reproduce that experience may have actually been the physical death of us. Remember, this wasn't a living room reno or even a whole home overhaul. This was another building over a hundred years old with surprises like needing steel beams brought in to support the sag of the building. And that was just for starters. Reviving an old building is like buying a mystery grab bag. You know something cool is inside, along with a lot of other stuff the clerk couldn't sell to anyone if they actually saw it. And for every gem of an old building you find, there are at least two major "uh-oh" surprises. It's just how a project like this goes. There's also the red tape of trying to take a building from the 1800s and bring it up to today's code. Still, we managed to pull off what had initially seemed impossible.

The space was the perfect canvas and one of our personal properties. That way, if nothing ever took off, we still had a finished product that was ours. Ben has always been at the helm of our renovation projects. To be sure, I offer input and we collaborate, but he's clearly the mastermind. I love to watch his vision take shape in shelled-out spaces. His countenance shifts as he considers possibilities with care. He mentally casts new walls within the barrenness, artfully arranges the lay of the land, engineers imagination to give form to desolation, draws up dreams from an unending well of creativity. In design shows, it's assumed that the wife decorates with all of the finishing touches. While it's antithetical to expectation, Ben does most projects on his own while I brush my hand across a dusty wall, hoping to reveal a remnant of the stories that were written there before we begin to write a new one.

Through the entire process, Ben and I were told to keep our expectations so low we could trip over them. It's like playing the lottery, they said. The chance of our pilot actually turning into a show was as unlikely as winning the Powerball. On the other hand, we were asked to begin the wondrous process of considering what kind of product lines we might want to one day endorse if the show took off. And we were encouraged to really think through if we would want to live a life of fame, should fate have it for us.

It was the strangest place in which to emotionally reside. And it added to the weirdness of everything about our Main Street living arrangements. We lived there but not really, with our Airbnb vagabond life. And the potential of the show tasted an awful lot like the "maybe" flavor of that experience; our house might feel like home but it was really not, and we might have a show and we might not, and we might taste national success and we might not. Couple the weight of unending workdays with toggling in between residences during the filming process and you can imagine how disconcerting it felt sometimes. In the middle of all this, I was also nursing my new sobriety, just five months old when this process started. I was feeling all the feels, facing it all without Merlot in my life anymore.

At no point during the process did I fall in love with the idea of being a television designer. On the contrary, I had some apprehension. If this took off, it would mean giving my time and giftings over to design, leaving little time for writing. The few hours left in a day would be protected for off-camera Ben and the girls, with no reserves for my own creative endeavors. But it also might be worth it if we had a platform that would provide the springboard for the projects that were dear to my own heart. For me it was always about an on-ramp for writing. Maybe if people knew who I was they might want to read my book. That possibility even took shape in the form of a conversation with a representative from Zondervan, an imprint of HarperCollins publishing. That aforementioned literary agent had been able to put together that call and for me, it was the carrot, the one thing I most wanted to chase from this whole project, an opportunity to write a book.

The experience of filming the pilot was nothing like I could have imagined, better than I ever expected, and more exhausting than I wanted to continue. In front of the camera, we talked about reimagining the space, taking it from shambles to a cozy, swanky loft. And when the cameras were off, we spent time with the crew. That was the best part. During the whole process, Ben and I were deeply grateful for the relationships that we formed. Other people's stories have always intrigued me, so I fed off a steady diet of new stories from new friends. It was invigorating and inspiring to be surrounded by so many creatives at one time. We made close friends along the way and some of them became our people. For life. Because of that, we came out prizewinners.

At the wrap of construction and filming, we held our breath while the team edited and re-edited. For six months we lived in limbo. We had conversations that toggled between, "Think about what you might do with your platform if this thing takes off," to "Remember, the actual chance of these things becoming a series is one in a million." So, for half a year, we were holding on to hope and hopelessness with equal grip. It's a strange place to inhabit.

Did we have the winning number? Was the show what HGTV was looking for? At the end of a prolonged wait, we got the answer we'd been prepped for but still felt the sharp sting of.

We didn't make the cut.

No show. Meaning no platform. Meaning no book deal. Meaning no new life-lane to open up for our family.

All of the sudden, Main Street seemed very small.

We regrouped pretty well. We had already returned to the rhythm of our normal life while waiting and had been living that way for months. Sure, there were looming question marks floating around our minds, but our day-to-day looked very much the same. When we got the news, I did what anyone in my situation might do. I headed to the grocery store and loaded my car with carbs and HGTV magazines and sat on the couch sulking for three days watching Netflix. Then we gathered our wits about us and went on about our lives as only one can after they have a brief encounter with what I came to think of as "The Almost."

Right as the news came in about the pilot not being picked up, I had just crossed over the one-year mark of sobriety. My sadness about the show could only last for so long, as I was living in the full swing of life and was determined to maintain that mindset. I wasn't about to let that HGTV *no* become a defining story in my life. My yes to sobriety was going to carry me into the next chapter, whatever that was.

My focus shifted from the continued renovation of Main Street to writing more in my own redemption story.

The Almost was a lot to process. It's not that I hadn't been through things in my life that were even tougher or more tragic. I had, and I knew that in the grand scheme of things, The Almost didn't compare. But it was still a dark several months, to say the least. It felt like I was walking around with lead in my limbs.

As it does, time began to melt the weight of disappointment over the show off my shoulders.

The summer after our production wrapped, I got a call from my friend Katye, the production company SVP. I figured she was calling with her friend hat on as we had become especially close and neither show outcome would have affected that. I answered expecting just to catch up. Instead, she called with an opportunity to basically try our hand at the jackpot, this time for Chip and Joanna Gaines' upcoming Magnolia network. It was a better fit for us than the HGTV show. The gist of this pitch kept Ben and I more true to our actual life story and included our design projects as they ran parallel to our Airbnb projects. It seemed to encompass our family more as a whole. It was the story of the Hardins, how we fell in love with our Shelbyville Main Street and our renovation projects in our hometown. We bit.

This time, the synopsis the production company created was more like a short film. Its voice was more authentic and its style was more true to us. With expectations still dragging the ground, we gave it our best shot. We loved everything about how it turned out. I felt like it just might take, but we held everything with loose fingers.

And then we get the call that we thought would change our lives. Chip and Joanna Gaines gave our project a thumbs up! We would begin filming in a couple of weeks. We started readying for everything, working out preliminary logistical details on projects, having strategic planning meetings, and I, of course, made sure to get my hair color freshened up. So, all the important things. It was our slow season for Airbnb travel, and we were going to be able to accommodate the crew between our properties for the first shooting. We were thrilled to be hosting the team we'd grown to care about so much!

Ben and I were getting things in order and keeping our emotions in check. Even though all signs indicated a full green light, we were still a little afraid to get excited. It just all felt surreal. I kept pinching myself. From time to time we would just look at each other and shrug with, "Like, really? This is really happening?" With filming a couple of weeks away, we finally let ourselves feel the thrill of it all. And we got swept up in the excitement.

Then, the other shoe dropped. Katye called. The production company president was on the phone with her as well. We could immediately tell by the sound in her voice that something was wrong. Shaky, she rushed past chit chat and told us that as baffling as it was, she had just gotten word that the whole thing was off. As is no go. As in, it was not happening.

All she knew was that either Chip or Joanna changed their mind.

They didn't know which one.

They didn't know why.

It was just over.

I remember just sitting there, limp. I felt like a sack of potatoes, heavy from rejection as I plunked down on the bed. Ben and I laid there without speaking for a long time. Could've been a minute. Could've been an hour. Everything felt frozen.

Another almost new beginning.

Another almost onramp for writing.

Another almost success.

But here's the thing. Pull up a chair so you can listen carefully. If we had gotten that TV spot, I would have had to put on a show for however many seasons of television life we were offered. You see, I was presented with the possibility of projecting an identity that a lot of people would die to have. But the thing is, that's not who I really am. I had bought into a story about my own life just because it was the leading headline. But as they say, there's always more to the story. And that's where I come in.

I had a dream of my own, one that wasn't predicated on the same one as my husband's. It had been hard to see because I kept it tucked away in the shadows, hard to see in the shine of the incredible light you could see, the thing we often called "our dream," the possibility of having a show.

And after that second Almost, instead of waiting for someone to create an opportunity for me, I decided it was time to make my dream my own.

It hasn't always been easy for me to navigate my own pursuits. I can easily slip into helper mode, making sure everyone else's dreams have fuel while neglecting to fill my own tank. But in the wake of these two earnest pursuits, followed by two crushing rejections, the gift it left me with was knowing it was time for me to step into my own passions.

My own creativity begged to be unleashed. My want for more self-identity kept nudging me. The magnetic lure of having something of my own began to pull me out from behind the curtain. I am finding my own way. Within our way. I didn't long for an out; I needed an "alongside." And so that's becoming our new flow.

Listen, I know the details of this are super specific, but there's something in here that I think we can all identify with on some level. We all tell stories about our life. Those plotlines that map out our individual or family narrative. Some of them are on loop because we love the telling of them. Some of them are just worn out. There is whisper just beneath the consistent conversation piece that could be the start of your next chapter.

COMING INTO
THE LIGHT

You know how when you're looking for your glasses and you find them on top of your head, or you're searching for your keys and all the while they are in your pocket? And you can't imagine how you ever could have had such trouble finding them?

One morning I came in from a run, glanced in the hall mirror, and stopped dead in my tracks. I tilted my head to the side and squinted to focus. I was flushed from my labored steps and the early sun. My hair was in a finger-combed ponytail, frazzled from being tossed about in the morning air. My skin was still layered in sweat, some dripping from my forehead. I wiped my brow and refocused. And then my eyes gradually widened to see myself as I hadn't in years.

I thought: *Oh!?! There you are. Right in front of me. I've been looking for you for so long. The friend in the mirror.*

My image and I shared a deep gaze, wordlessly recounting all our memories together, wondering how we ever lost touch. I looked at the familiar stranger for a long time. I tried to remember exactly what happened to her. How had I relegated her to keep behind the glass?

I suppose I chased the baits of productivity and pleasing, and eventually outpaced all but a fading reflection of my true self. Out here beyond the rectangle frame, I had layered the importance of others' opinions on top of her, and the real me was suffocating. I had busied myself outside of myself to such the point that I nearly lost myself.

But there she was. And once I saw her again, I couldn't deny she was there. Or that she was trapped.

While at first I felt immense grief, intrigue and eventually excitement followed. I knew I could free her. I could be her. Because I already was her. I just wasn't sure how to meld our worlds together—the ones separated by expectation.

It took some time, but I mustered up every bit of courage I had forgotten was mine. I began to dismantle the deep seeded beliefs that doing enough equaled being enough. Sometimes I still forget. But when I do, I stop and lock eyes with the girl in the mirror and tell her, "Don't you dare go anywhere."

Epilogue

Y ou can see it coming from miles away.

It is not random or unexpected. There are signs that point to the coming of an eclipse and they are so precise that we can count on it beyond a shadow of a doubt. Like set your watch and bust out the backyard blankets and solar viewers.

It's happening in 3, 2, 1.

Just as an eclipse is reliant upon the cyclical alignment of the Earth, moon and sun, so too can we likely trace the patterns of our own personal placement along the constellation of life choices and circumstances that led to the eclipsing of our souls time and again. Sure, maybe we can't pinpoint the exact moment when the shadows swallow us, but we can sense the fading away of ourselves until we've nearly vanished.

Sometimes the eclipse is partial. The shadow of the moon is not big enough to overwhelm all of Earth, so it is limited to only part of the planet. Likewise, in those seasons, we are beaming for the most part but a shroud covers an area or areas of our lives. We've all been there, right?

Other times we can see an outline of ourselves, blazing in some periphery areas of life but blacked out in the core of our being, like a ring of fire eclipse. In those seasons, we are bright and bold in the world but dim the minute we walk into the core of our personal stories.

There may be a few pages in certain chapters of our lives that are almost completely obstructed by gloom. It can be hard to remember what radiance is at all.

But we don't have to face the far side of the moon forever.

You see, the Light drew me in, outrivaling the shadows of my story.

It was there all along.

Inside of me.

Not out there in the universe somewhere above the cosmos, but within me.

And it's in all of us, too.

God's light eclipses all of our collective darkness and it shines through all of our collective light.

And because God is Light, and we are God's, we are uneclipsed.

Acknowledgments

A few years ago, I began to resign to the fact that the fingerprints I was going to leave as my legacy were going to be smudged helping turn the pages of others' stories instead of actually telling (or living) my own. I tried to settle into that, to quiet the whispers of my heart. Until I just couldn't anymore. In the global slowdown from the pandemic, those soul whispers began to raise their voice until I had to give them an audience. The fear of telling my stories became eclipsed by the bigger fear of breaking my own heart by not writing the book that had been stirring within me for years.

It's always been a weird thing to me to say that I'm a writer. I sort of pass it off and shuffle my feet and offer, "Well, I mean I like to write too," when people ask me about my hobbies. I've had success as a former corporate sales rep, wellness coach, entrepreneur, real estate agent, and a few other professional titles. It was easy to announce those things. But they were just what I did, not who I am.

I'm finally stepping into the truth of a huge part of my identity, that I *am* a writer.

These are the names of those who have helped write this story in one way or another. Some have directly impacted this work and others have directly impacted the me who was able to write it.

Ben: My love, you are so easy to admire. Your audacity has fueled my boldness to step into my own dreams. You have been a constant voice of support in this. There's no one I'd rather be doing this wild ride of a life with but you. It's us forever.

Mama: You said years ago that I would write a book when I found my story. Well, I suppose you were right after all (no surprise). Thank you for being such an encouragement along the way. I learned to pen my thoughts by watching you weave your words into the pages of countless notebooks that hold so many of your own stories. Your voracious appetite for learning has spurred the exploration of my own curiosities. I'm so glad you're my Mama.

Daddy: I'm not sure how this works, but I feel like my soul seamlessly heard the chorus of heaven through angels and then the music of earth through your voice. Because of you, I have never lived in a world without song. That's a gift that's meant more to me than you could know. Watching you walk in your gifts has fueled me with both the want and the example to do the same. I treasure you.

Julie Lyles Carr: You fashioned the latticework for my words, helping me to interlace the details of my story onto a framework that supported both my authentic voice as well as the reader's experience. You are a fusion of hilarity and humility, wisdom and warmth, enlightenment and empowerment. I'm both in awe of you and of the gift it is to know you. If I could sew, I'd make you a cape that reads: Wizardess of Wordsmithery.

Whitney: You've been gently and patiently entertaining my false starts for a few years now and have been so gracious with your time to help me sort through the layers of this project. I'm extremely appreciative of your kindness and candor. Your savvy and sharp business acumen are coupled with your soft heart and I just respect you so much. I'm deeply grateful for your guidance, expertise, and friendship.

My Tribe—Bethany, Malia, Tiffany, and Rachel: I'm so grateful to be encircled within our friendship. You have been my lifelines in so many chapters of life. Bethany, you are a real-life missionary who lives to serve behind the scenes and whose warmth could literally mend a broken heart. Malia, you are the metronome whose hallmark is your steadiness of soul. Tiff, your trademark is your fierce love for your people and I'm of the firm belief that you could do literally anything you put your mind to as your tenacity and energy reserves are endless. Rachel, your spirit and your smile could rule the Commonwealth (and actually may one day). You could fill a room with your framed accomplishments but live with a humble heart and make time for soul-deep connection with people. A very special thanks to you for the literal years you've nudged me to write this book, for being relentless in your encouragement and for graciously reading so many rough drafts.

Lee: So grateful for your promptings to take this chance. And for a lifelong friendship of sincere care for one another. Thankful for our conversations full of healthy tension and respect, each one ending with a hug and "love you, friend." I sure do.

Stacy and Melissa: Our roundtable readings were a welcome mat for my vulnerability, a rally for my bravery, and an affirmation of my authorship. Thank you for sharing sneak previews of your incredible work with me. I am blown away by the unique gift of writing you both possess. Just wow.

Katye: My sister of serendipity. We thought we were meeting about a television show. Instead, we get to be in the real-life stories of each other's lives forever. Your embodiment of the spirit of Christ is a connector for me to Jesus. You are an activator of faith and dreams and joy. I'm so deeply grateful to be your friend.

Lisa: You have been church to me in so many ways. You've helped me work out some pretty big splinters, all the while holding my heart with tender care. There are so many parts of this book that are offshoots of our MPs. You are a well of wisdom and insight, a true sojourner, and a loyal friend.

Lewis: I feel like I'm bragging when I tell people we're related. The doting little sister, I'm just wildly crazy about you. Watching you live out your gift of music has always inspired me. Love you so much.

Lee and Londi: When I was floundering in fear, you put your hand on my shoulder and assured me I could not lose God. Always love our (however infrequent) conversations of curiosity and wonder.

Lea: I'm so grateful that our lives intersected and for our insistence in authentic friendship. Thank you so much for putting eyes on this work in its roughest form and for offering such insightful feedback.

Jeannine: Who knew when I rolled up into your office that I'd just hit the jackpot?! You wrote my heart permission slips to show itself in its entirety and have been a guiding light on my path.

Leslie: The potency of our connection is so rich and real, even if only tended to through visits that are too far apart and never long enough and phone calls that are often inter-rupted. Ours is a special bond. You are so dear to me, my sister-cousin-friend. Also, your laughter should be bottled and sold. It's pure gold.

Amy: You said not to mention your name in the book, but I took liberty to do it at least here as you are namelessly sprinkled throughout the pages. I'd be remiss not to thank you. You

ACKNOWLEDGMENTS

have been a big sister and mentor to me. Your no-nonsense guidance is so helpful to my overthinking personality. I can always count on your ability to see clearly where I'm cloudy. I just adore you.

Cynthia: Every time I'm with you I feel a sweet nearness to the heart of God. You radiate light and draw people into their best selves. Thank you for being my friend.

Nikki and Emily: I've never laughed so hard as when I'm with you. I could write a whole other book full of the stories we've lived and shared over fifteen years of spaghetti dinners. I love you both so much, and it's all for free.

Author Biography

M ELINDA HARDIN is a well-rounded plate spinner who is fueled by the diversity of her many roles.

Professionally, she is a multi-space Airbnb host, a successful real estate agent, an event space owner, and an entrepreneurial partner with her husband Ben on several historic building projects. She is also a singer in a band, *The Pretty Goods*, a contributing writer for her hometown magazine, and a yoga instructor.

Along the road of her professional career, she has been a pharmaceutical sales rep, a wellness coach, a corporate wellness director, birth doula, and restaurateur. A student at heart, it's not uncommon to find Melinda with her nose in a book or registering for a new class. As such, she has completed several fitness and wellness certifications and holds a master's degree in Holistic Wellness. All courses considered, her greatest teachers continue to be her two daughters, Annie and Celia. She's also a former booze enthusiast but now spends her days celebrating her sobriety, eyes wide open and all in on this adventure of life.

The whisper of her heart, along with her friends and family, nudged her to write this book for years. Her collection of morning pages, backs of napkins, twelve-step worksheets, and sticky notes took shape into themes, and those themes took on the formation of chapters, and those chapters found their way into this book.

You can find this book and more at

www.melindamhardin.com
and follow Melinda on Instagram (@melindamhardin)
and on Facebook as Melinda Hardin.

Or you can stop by Main Street in Shelbyville, Kentucky. She's usually around there somewhere and would love to chat over a cup of coffee.

Notes

1   "Solar Eclipse." Wikipedia. Wikimedia Foundation, October 10, 2021. https://en.wikipedia.org/wiki/Solar_eclipse.

2   Dale Carnegie, *How to Win Friends and Influence People*. (Pocketbooks, 1998).

3   Cummings, E. E. (n.d.). *E.E. Cummings quote: "yours is the light by which my spirit's born: – you are my sun, My Moon, and all my stars."*. Quotefancy. Retrieved January 14, 2022, from https://quotefancy.com/quote/6307/E-E-Cummings-Yours-is-the-light-by-which-my-spirit-s-born-you-are-my-sun-my-moon-and-all

4   Center for Action and Contemplation daily meditation. Tuesday, March 29, 2016. Changing Our Minds Fr. Richard Rohr, OFM

5   Rainer Maria Rilke, Letters to a Young Poet. (Hythloday Press, 2014), Poem 4.

6   Patty Griffin, "When It Don't Come Easy," April 20, 2004, Track #8 on Impossible Dream, ATO Records, 2004, album.

7   Bill Gaither Trio, "I Am a Promise," 1979, Track A2 on I Am a

Promise, Word Record, 1979, album.

8 Rumi. "A Great Wagon," *Rumi: Selected Poems*, translated by Coleman Barks, with John Moynce, A. J. Arberry, Reynold Nicholson (London: Penguin, 2004).